The blind Milton dictating *Paradise Lost* to his daughters.

From the painting of Munkacsy.

The Academy Classics

PARADISE LOST

Books I and II

EDITED BY

HENRY W. BOYNTON

ALLYN AND BACON

Boston New York Chicago

Norwood Press
J. S. Cushing Co. — Berwick & Smith Co.
Norwood, Mass., U.S.A.

INTRODUCTION.

It is doubtless possible to study the first two books of *Paradise Lost* by themselves with some degree of profit. They have a unity of their own. The limited field of action, the strength and simplicity of the conception which we here get of Satan and his followers, the dramatic quality of the dialogue (which seldom lapses into mere declamation), — all these characteristics of this fragment give it an interest of its own. And yet, after all, it is only a fragment. We must go back of, and forward of, these events in order to grasp their full meaning. Here is pictured the noblest phase of Satan's nature, but it is a phase which is to be succeeded by other developments of no less interest. The episode of the interview with Sin and Death is mainly significant as a prophecy: these monsters become of importance only in the sequel. Hell is here the stage of action; but there was a former and more varied action on the greater stage of Heaven, and there is to be a later (and again more active) series of events on the lesser stage of Earth.

We shall attempt to trace from beginning to end the course of that great story of which the first two books constitute an intermediate episode. And we shall begin by quoting somewhat freely from Masson, the greatest of Milton's editors (*Introduction to Paradise Lost*, pp. 26–30): —

'*Paradise Lost* is an epic. But it is not, like the Iliad or the Æneid, a national epic; nor is it an epic after any other of the known types. It is an epic of the whole human species, an epic of our entire planet, or indeed of the entire astronomical universe. The title of the poem, though perhaps the best that could have been chosen, hardly indicates beforehand the full nature or extent of the theme; nor are the opening lines, by themselves, sufficiently descriptive of what is to follow. According to them, the story is to be

> "Of Man's first disobedience, and the fruit
> Of that forbidden tree whose mortal taste
> Brought death into the world, and all our woe,
> With loss of Eden."

This is a true enough description, because the whole story bears on this point. But it is the vast comprehension of the story, both in space and in time, as leading to this point, that makes it unique among epics, and entitles Milton to speak of it as involving

> "Things unattempted yet in prose or rhyme."

It is, in short, a poetical representation, on the authority of hints from the Book of Genesis, of the historical connection between Human Time and Aboriginal or Eternal Infinity, or between our created World and the immeasurable and inconceivable Universe of Pre-human Existence. So far as our World is concerned, the poem starts from that moment when our newly-created Earth, with all the newly-created starry depths about it, had as yet but two human beings upon it; and these consequently are, on this side of the pre-supposed Infinite Eternity, the main persons of the epic. But we are carried back *into* this pre-supposed Infinite Eternity, and the grand purpose of the poem is to connect, by a stupendous imagination, certain events or courses of the inconceivable history that had been unfolding itself there with the first fortunes of that new azure World which is familiar to us, and more particularly with the first fortunes of that favored ball at the centre whereon those two human creatures walked. Now the person of the epic through the narration of whose acts this connection is established is Satan. He, as all critics have perceived, and in a wider sense than most of them have perceived, is the real hero of the poem. He and his actions are the link between that new World of Man the infancy of which we behold in the poem, and that boundless antecedent Universe of Prehuman Existence which the poem assumes. For he was a native of that Pre-human Universe, — one of its greatest and most conspicuous natives; and what we follow in the poem, when its story is taken chronologically, is the life of this great being, from the time of his yet unimpaired primacy or archangelship among the Celestials, on to that time when, in pursuit of a scheme of revenge, he flings himself into the new experimental World, tries the strength of the new race at its fountain-head, and, by success in his attempt, vitiates Man's portion of space to his own nature, and wins possession of it for a season.

'Aboriginally, or in primeval Eternity, before the creation of our Earth or the Starry Universe to which it belongs, universal space is to be considered, according to the requisites of the poem, not as containing stars or starry systems at all, but as, so to say, a sphere of infinite radius, divided equatorially into two hemispheres, thus:

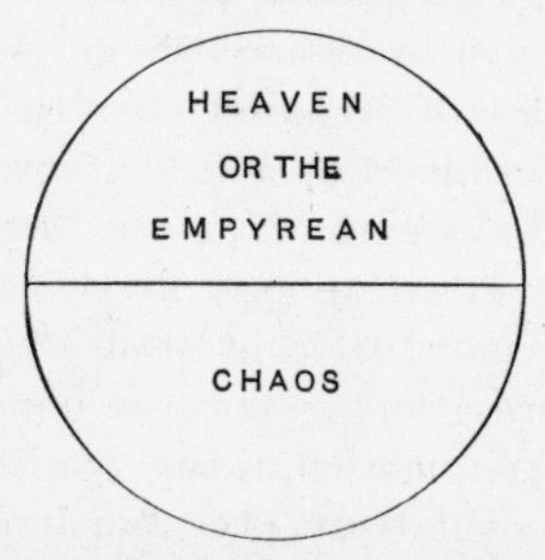

The upper of these two hemispheres of primeval Infinity is Heaven, or The Empyrean, — a boundless, unimaginable region of Light, Freedom, Happiness, and Glory, in the midst whereof Deity, though omnipresent, has His immediate and visible dwelling, and where He is surrounded by a vast population of beings, called "the Angels," or "Sons of God," who draw near to His throne in worship, derive thence their nurture and their delight, and yet live dispersed through all the ranges and recesses of the region, leading severally their mighty lives and performing the behests of Deity, but organized into companies, orders, and hierarchies. Milton is careful to explain that all he says of Heaven is said symbolically, and in order to make conceivable by the human imagination what in its own nature is inconceivable; but, this explained, he is bold enough in his use of terrestrial analogies. Round the immediate throne of Deity, indeed, there is kept a blazing mist of vagueness, which words are hardly permitted to pierce, though the Angels are represented as from time to time assembling within it, beholding the Divine Presence and hearing the Divine Voice. But Heaven at large, or portions of it, are figured as tracts of a celestial Earth, with plain, hill, and valley, wherein the myriads of the Sons of God expatiate, in their two orders of Seraphim and Cherubim, and in their descending ranks as Archangels or Chiefs, Princes of various degrees, and individual Powers and Intelligences. Certain differences, however, are implied as distinguishing these Celestials from the subsequent race of Mankind. As they are of infinitely greater prowess, immortal, and of more purely spiritual nature, so their ways even of physical existence and action transcend all that is within human experience. Their forms are dilatable or contractible at pleasure; they move with incredible swiftness; and as they are not subject to any law of gravitation, their motion, though ordinarily represented as horizontal over the Heavenly ground, may as well be vertical or in any other direction, and their aggregations need not, like those of men, be in squares, oblongs, or other plane figures, but may be in cubes, or other rectangular or oblique solids, or in spherical masses. . . . As respects the other half or hemisphere of the primeval Infinity, though it too is inconceivable in its nature, and has to be described by words which are at best symbolical, less needs be said. For it is CHAOS, or the Uninhabited,—a huge, limitless ocean, abyss, or quagmire, of universal darkness and lifelessness, wherein are jumbled in blustering confusion the elements of all matter, or rather the crude embryons of all the elements, ere as yet they are distinguishable. There is no light there, nor properly Earth, Water, Air, or Fire, but only a vast pulp or welter of unformed matter, in which all these lie tempestuously intermixed. Though the presence of Deity is there potentially too, it is still, as it were, actually retracted thence, as from a realm unorganized and left to Night and Anarchy; nor do any of the Angels wing down into its repulsive obscurities. The crystal floor or wall of Heaven divides them from it; underneath which, and unvisited of light, save what may glimmer through upon its nearer strata, it howls and rages and stagnates eternally. —Such is and has been the constitution of the Universal Infinitude from ages immemorial in the Angelic reckoning.'

But such was not to be the final constitution either of the cosmogony or of the Heavenly society; for on a day,

On such day
As Heaven's great year brings forth, the empyreal host
Of Angels, by imperial summons called,
Innumerable before the Almighty's throne
Forthwith from all the ends of Heaven appeared
Under their Hierarchs in order bright:
Ten thousand thousand ensigns high advanced,
Standards and gonfalons, 'twixt van and rear
Stream in the air, and for distinction serve
Of hierarchies, of orders, and degrees;

Or in their glittering tissues bear emblazed
Holy memorials, acts of zeal and love
Recorded eminent. Thus when in orbs
Of circuit inexpressible they stood,
Orb within orb, the Father Infinite,
By whom in bliss imbosomed sat the Son,
Amidst as from a flaming mount, whose top
Brightness had made invisible, thus spake: —
'Hear, all ye Angels, progeny of light,
Thrones, Dominations, Princedoms, Virtues, Powers,
Hear my decree, which unrevoked shall stand:
This day I have begot whom I declare
My only Son; and on this holy hill
Him have anointed, whom ye now behold
At my right hand. Your Head I him appoint;
And by myself have sworn, to him shall bow
All knees in Heaven, and shall confess him Lord:
Under his great vicegerent reign abide,
United as one individual soul,
Forever happy. Him who disobeys,
Me disobeys, breaks union, and that day
Cast out from God and blessed vision, falls
Into utter darkness, deep engulfed, his place
Ordained without redemption, without end.'
So spake the Omnipotent; and with his words
All seemed well pleased; all seemed, but were not all.

(V. 582-617.)

The day which follows is employed, like all former Heavenly days, in songs, dancing, and feasting:

Secure
Of surfeit, where full measure only bounds
Excess, before the All-bounteous King, who showered
With copious hand, rejoicing in their joy.
Now when ambrosial Night, with clouds exhaled
From that high mount of God, whence light and shade
Spring both, the face of brightest Heaven had changed
To grateful twilight (for Night comes not there

In darker veil), and roseate dews disposed
All but the unsleeping eyes of God to rest:
Wide over all the plain, and wider far
Than all this globous Earth in plain outspread
(Such are the courts of God), the Angelic throng,
Dispersed in bands and files, their camp extend
By living streams among the trees of life:
Pavilions numberless, and sudden reared,
Celestial tabernacles, where they slept
Fanned with cool winds; save those who in their course
Melodious hymns about the sovran throne
Alternate all night long. But not so waked
Satan; so call him now, his former name
Is heard no more in Heaven. He of the first,
If not the first Archangel, great in power,
In favor, and pre-eminence, yet fraught
With envy against the Son of God, that day
Honored by his great Father, and proclaimed
Messiah, King Anointed, could not bear
Through pride that sight, and thought himself impaired.
Deep malice thence conceiving, and disdain,
Soon as midnight brought on the dusky hour
Friendliest to sleep and silence, he resolved
With all his legions to dislodge, and leave
Unworshipped, unobeyed the Throne supreme,
Contemptuous. (V. 638–671.)

He awakes his 'next subordinate,' Beelzebub, and, plainly insinuating his purpose of rebellion, proposes that an assembly be made 'of all those myriads which we lead in chief,' ostensibly to prepare for the reception of the son (called in this passage 'the great Messiah'), who is soon to make his initial progress of royal pomp through his dominions. Beelzebub is instantly at work. He advises 'the regent powers, under him regent,' of Satan's will

Tells the suggested cause, and casts between
Ambiguous words and jealousies, to sound

Or taint integrity. But all obeyed
The wonted signal and superior voice
Of their great potentate; for great indeed
His name, and high was his degree in Heaven:
His countenance as the morning star that guides
The starry flock, allured them, and with lies
Drew after him the third part of Heaven's host.
Meanwhile the Eternal Eye, whose sight discerns
Abstrusest thoughts, from forth his holy mount,
And from within the golden lamps that burn
Nightly before him, saw without their light
Rebellion rising; saw in whom, how spread
Among the Sons of Morn, what multitudes
Were banded to oppose his high decree.

(V. 702–717.)

The Father and the Son commune with regard to the threatened uprising, and we are given to know at the outset that it is all a part of the divine plan. In the meantime Satan's host is assembling,

Innumerable as the stars of night,
Or stars of morning, dewdrops, which the sun
Impearls on every leaf and every flower.

(V. 745–747.)

At last they come into the far north, and to the abode of Satan, which Milton himself calls a 'royal seat':

High on a hill, far blazing, as a mount
Raised on a mount, with pyramids and towers
From diamond quarries hewn, and rocks of gold.

(V. 757–759.)

Satan from his throne addresses them, at first in a stately strain not unlike that in which the Father himself has spoken; but soon with a rush of feeling:

'Thrones, Dominations, Princedoms, Virtues, Powers, —
If these magnific titles yet remain

Not merely titular, since by decree
Another now hath to himself ingrossed
All power, and us eclipsed under the name
Of King Anointed; for whom all this haste
Of midnight march, and hurried meeting here,
This only to consult, how we may best,
With what may be devised of honors new,
Receive him coming to receive from us
Knee-tribute yet unpaid, prostration vile!
Too much to one! but double how endured —
To one and to his image now proclaimed?
But what if better counsels might erect
Our minds, and teach us to cast off this yoke?
Will ye submit your necks, and choose to bend
The supple knee? Ye will not, if I trust
To know ye right; or if ye know yourselves
Natives and Sons of Heaven possessed before
By none, and, if not equal all, yet free,
Equally free; for orders and degrees
Jar not with liberty, but well consist.
Who can in reason then or right assume
Monarchy over such as live by right
His equals — if in power and splendor less,
In freedom equal? or can introduce
Law and edict on us, who without law
Err not? much less for this to be our Lord,
And look for adoration, to the abuse
Of those imperial titles which assert
Our being ordained to govern, not to serve!'

(V. 772–802.)

The appeal is heard with favor by all but one, the Seraph Abdiel, who, after a fiery protest against Satan's infidelity, and a strict defence of the divine right, finds himself still alone in his position. Satan inquires ironically for proof that the angels owe their being to God:

'Remember'st thou
Thy making, while the Maker gave thee being?

We know no time when we were not as now;
Know none before us, self-begot, self-raised
By our own quickening power, when fatal course
Had circled his full orb; the birth mature
Of this our native Heaven, Ethereal Sons.
Our puissance is our own; our own right hand
Shall teach us highest deeds, by proof to try
Who is our equal: then thou shalt behold
Whether by supplication we intend
Address, and to begirt the Almighty Throne
Beseeching or besieging. This report,
These tidings, carry to the Anointed King;
And fly, ere evil intercept thy flight.'
He said; and as the sound of waters deep,
Hoarse murmur echoed to his words applause
Through the infinite host.

(V. 857-874.)

The challenge is given. Abdiel, flinging them a prophecy of their fall, goes out from them:

Among the faithless, faithful only he;
Among innumerable false, unmoved,
Unshaken, unseduced, unterrified,
His loyalty he kept, his love, his zeal;
Nor numbers, nor example, with him wrought
To swerve from truth, or change his constant mind,
Though single. From amidst them forth he passed,
Long way through hostile scorn, which he sustained
Superior, nor of violence feared aught;
And with retorted scorn his back he turned
On those proud towers, to swift destruction doomed.

(V. 897-907.)

He pursues his way to the sacred regions of God's nearer presence, and finds his news already known, and preparations for war already made. From the cloud which hangs over the sacred hill comes the mild voice of God in commendation of his faithful servant, to whom he promises an easier task in the subduing by force of the rebellious crew. Michael is made commander-in-chief, with Gabriel as his lieutenant, and bidden drive Satan and his followers out of Heaven

'Into their place of punishment, the gulf
Of Tartarus, which ready opens wide
His fiery Chaos to receive their fall.'
 So spake the Sovran Voice; and clouds began
To darken all the hill, and smoke to roll
In dusky wreaths reluctant flames, the sign
Of wrath awaked; nor with less dread the loud
Ethereal trumpet from on high 'gan blow:
At which command the powers militant
That stood for Heaven, in mighty quadrate joined
Of union irresistible, moved on
In silence their bright legions, to the sound
Of instrumental harmony, that breathed
Heroic ardor to adventurous deeds
Under their godlike leaders, in the cause
Of God and his Messiah. On they move
Indissolubly firm: nor obvious hill,
Nor straitening vale, nor wood, nor stream, divides
Their perfect ranks; for high above the ground
Their march was, and the passive air upbore
Their nimble tread. As when the total kind
Of birds, in orderly array on wing,
Came summoned over Eden, to receive
Their names of thee*; so over many a tract
Of Heaven they marched, and many a province wide
Tenfold the length of this terrene. At last,
Far in the horizon to the north appeared
From skirt to skirt a fiery region, stretched
In battailous aspect, and nearer view
Bristled with upright beams innumerable
Of rigid spears, and helmets thronged, and shields
Various, with boastful argument portrayed;

* Raphael is telling the story to Adam.

The banded Powers of Satan hasting on
With furious expedition; for they weened
That self-same day, by fight or by surprise,
To win the Mount of God, and on his throne
To set the envier of his state, the proud
Aspirer; but their thoughts proved fond and vain
In the mid-way. Though strange to us it seemed
At first, that Angel should with Angel war,
And in fierce hosting meet, who wont to meet
So oft in festivals of joy and love
Unanimous, as sons of one great Sire,
Hymning the Eternal Father; but the shout
Of battle now began, and rushing sound
Of onset ended soon each milder thought.
High in the midst, exalted as a God,
The Apostate in his sun-bright chariot sat,
Idol of majesty divine, enclosed
With flaming Cherubim and golden shields;
Then lighted from his gorgeous throne; for now
'Twixt host and host but narrow space was left
(A dreadful interval), and front to front
Presented stood, in terrible array,
Of hideous length. Before the cloudy van,
On the rough edge of battle ere it joined,
Satan, with vast and haughty strides advanced,
Came towering, armed in adamant and gold.

(VI. 53–110.)

Satan is at once confronted by the faithful Abdiel, whose words of contempt and defiance are flung back by the rebel Angel with bitter scorn. Abdiel answers his charges of servility and meanness of spirit, with magnificent firmness, concluding triumphantly:

'This is servitude,
To serve the unwise, or him who hath rebelled
Against his worthier, as thine now serve thee,
Thyself not free, but to thyself enthralled;

Yet lewdly darest our ministering upbraid.
Reign thou in Hell, thy kingdom; let me serve
In Heaven God ever blest, and his divine
Behests obey, worthiest to be obeyed;
Yet chains in Hell, not realms expect: meanwhile
From me returned, as erst thou saidst, from flight,
This greeting on thy impious crest receive.'
  So saying, a noble stroke he lifted high,
Which hung not, but so swift with tempest fell
On the proud crest of Satan, that no sight,
Nor motion of swift thought, less could his shield
Such ruin intercept. Ten paces huge
He back recoiled; the tenth on bended knee
His massy spear upstayed: as if on earth
Winds under ground, or waters forcing way
Sidelong, had pushed a mountain from his seat,
Half sunk with all his pines. Amazement seized
The rebel Thrones, but greater rage, to see
Thus foiled their mightiest; ours joy filled and shout,
Presage of victory and fierce desire
Of battle; whereat Michael bid sound
The Archangel trumpet: through the vast of Heaven
It sounded, and the faithful armies rung
Hosannah to the Highest: nor stood at gaze
The adverse legions, nor less hideous joined
The horrid shock. Now storming fury rose,
And clamor such as heard in Heaven till now
Was never; arms on armor clashing brayed
Horrible discord, and the madding wheels
Of brazen chariots raged; dire was the noise
Of conflict; overhead the dismal hiss
Of fiery darts in flaming volleys flew,
And flying vaulted either host with fire.
So under fiery cope together rushed
Both battles main with ruinous assault
And inextinguishable rage. All Heaven
Resounded; and had Earth been then, all Earth
Had to her centre shook.

(VI. 178-219.)

The hosts of Satan advance in apparently impregnable array:

> Each warrior single as in chief; expert
> When to advance, or stand, or turn the sway
> Of battle, open when, and when to close
> The ridges of grim war: no thought of flight,
> None of retreat; no unbecoming deed
> That argued fear: each on himself relied
> As only in his arm the moment lay
> Of victory. Deeds of eternal fame
> Were done, but infinite; for wide was spread
> That war, and various: sometimes on firm ground
> A standing fight; then, soaring on main wing,
> Tormented all the air; all air seemed then
> Conflicting fire. Long time in even scale
> The battle hung; till Satan, who that day
> Prodigious power had shown, and met in arms
> No equal, ranging through the dire attack
> Of fighting Seraphim confused, at length
> Saw where the sword of Michael smote, and felled
> Squadrons at once; with huge two-handed sway
> Brandished aloft, the horrid edge came down
> Wide wasting: such destruction to withstand
> He hasted, and opposed the rocky orb
> Of tenfold adamant, his ample shield,
> A vast circumference.
>
> (VI. 233–256.)

The armies withdraw, and leave the champions face to face. There is another wordy war, and at last

> They ended parle, and both addressed for fight
> Unspeakable; for who, though with the tongue
> Of Angels, can relate, or to what things
> Liken on Earth conspicuous, that may lift
> Human imagination to such highth
> Of godlike power? for likest gods they seemed,
> Stood they or moved, in stature, motion, arms;

Fit to decide the empire of great Heaven.
Now waved their fiery swords, and in the air
Made horrid circles: two broad suns their shields
Blazed opposite, while Expectation stood
In horror: from each hand with speed retired,
Where erst was thickest fight, the Angelic throng,
And left large field, unsafe within the wind
Of such commotion; such as, to set forth
Great things by small, if Nature's concord broke,
Among the constellations war were sprung,
Two planets rushing from aspect malign
Of fiercest opposition in mid-sky
Should combat, and their jarring spheres confound.
Together both, with next to almighty arm
Uplifted imminent, one stroke they aimed
That might determine, and not need repeat,
As not of power at once; nor odds appeared
In might or swift prevention. But the sword
Of Michael from the armory of God,
Was given him tempered so, that neither keen
Nor solid might resist that edge: it met
The sword of Satan with steep force to smite
Descending, and in half cut sheer; nor stayed,
But with swift wheel reverse, deep entering shared
All his right side. Then Satan first knew pain,
And writhed him to and fro convolved; so sore
The griding sword with discontinuous wound
Passed through him: but the ethereal substance closed,
Not long divisible; and from the gash
A stream of nectarous humor, issuing, flowed
Sanguine, such as celestial Spirits may bleed,
And all his armor stained, erewhile so bright.
Forthwith on all sides to his aid was run
By Angels many and strong, who interposed
Defence, while others bore him on their shields
Back to his chariot, where it stood retired
From off the files of war: there they him laid
Gnashing for anguish, and despite, and shame,
To find himself not matchless, and his pride

Humbled in that rebuke, so far beneath
His confidence to equal God in power.

(VI. 296–343.)

Satan is disabled for the moment: his followers share his reverse of fortune, and the first day closes with a nominal victory for the hosts of God.

The second day's struggle assumes Titanic proportions. It is no longer to be an orderly hand-to-hand struggle. Satan calls in the use of artillery. The army of God in desperation throw aside their arms

. . . And to the hills,
Light as the lightning-glimpse, they ran, they flew:
From their foundations, loosening to and fro,
They plucked the seated hills, with all their load,
Rocks, waters, woods, and by their shaggy tops
Uplifting, bore them in their hands.

(VI. 639–647.)

Satan's artillery is overwhelmed; and his followers, desperate in their turn, have recourse to the same tremendous weapons:

Infernal noise! War seemed a civil game
To this uproar: horrid confusion heaped
Upon confusion rose: and now all Heaven
Had gone to wrack, with ruin overspread,
Had not the Almighty Father, where he sits
Shrined in his sanctuary of Heaven secure,
Consulting on the sum of things, foreseen
This tumult, and permitted all, advised;
That his great purpose he might so fulfil,
To honor his Anointed Son, avenged
Upon his enemies, and to declare
All power on him transferred.

(VI. 667–678.)

The Son, endued with God's own omnipotence, pledges his willing service in the restoration of peace to Heaven by the overthrow and expulsion of the rebel crew.

And the third sacred morn began to shine,
Dawning thro' Heaven. Forth rushed with whirlwind sound
The chariot of Paternal Deity.

(VI. 748–751.)

* * * * * * * *

He, in celestial panoply all armed
Of radiant Urim, work divinely wrought,
Ascended. At his right hand victory
Sat eagle-winged; beside him hung his bow
And quiver with three-bolted thunder stored;
And from about him fierce effusion rolled
Of smoke and bickering flame and sparkles dire:
Attended with ten thousand thousand Saints,
He onward came; far off his coming shone;
And twenty thousand (I their number heard)
Chariots of God, half on each hand, were seen.
He on the wings of Cherub rode sublime
On the crystalline sky, in sapphire throned,
Illustrious far and wide, but by his own
First seen; them unexpected joy surprised,
When the great ensign of Messiah blazed
Aloft, by Angels borne, his sign in Heaven;
Under whose conduct Michael soon reduced
His army, circumfused on either wing,
Under their Head embodied all in one.
Before him power divine his way prepared:
At his command the uprooted hills retired
Each to his place; they heard his voice, and went
Obsequious; Heaven his wonted face renewed,
And with fresh flowerets hill and valley smiled.

(VI. 760–784.)

The rebel host perceive his coming with dismay, but stand resolute, determined to maintain their cause to the end. The Messiah addresses the faithful army of God; commends them for their fidelity and zeal, and shows them that it is fitting for him, the cause of the rebellion, the object of Satan's enmity, to be the instrument of God's power in restoring order and unanimity in Heaven.

So spake the Son, and into terror changed
His countenance, too severe to be beheld,
And full of wrath bent on his enemies.
At once the Four spread out their starry wings
With dreadful shade contiguous, and the orbs
Of his fierce chariot rolled, as with the sound
Of torrent floods, or of a numerous host.
He on his impious foes right onward drove,
Gloomy as night: under his burning wheels
The steadfast Empyrean shook throughout,
All but the throne itself of God. Full soon
Among them he arrived; in his right hand
Grasping ten thousand thunders, which he sent
Before him, such as in their souls infixed
Plagues. They, astonished, all resistance lost,
All courage; down their idle weapons dropt;
O'er shields and helms and helmed heads he rode
Of Thrones and mighty Seraphim prostrate,
That wished the mountains now might be again
Thrown on them, as a shelter from his ire.
Nor less on either side tempestuous fell
His arrows, from the fourfold-visaged Four,
Distinct with eyes, and from the living wheels
Distinct alike with multitude of eyes;
One Spirit in them ruled, and every eye
Glared lightning, and shot forth pernicious fire
Among the accursed, that withered all their strength,
And of their wonted vigor left them drained,
Exhausted, spiritless, afflicted, fallen:
Yet half his strength he put not forth, but checked
His thunder in mid-volley; for he meant
Not to destroy, but root them out of Heaven.
The overthrown he raised, and, as a herd
Of goats or timorous flock together thronged,

Drove them before him thunder struck, pursued
With terrors and with furies to the bounds
And crystal wall of Heaven; which opening wide,
Rolled inward, and a spacious gap disclosed
Into the wasteful Deep. The monstrous sight
Struck them with horror backward; but far worse
Urged them behind; headlong themselves they threw
Down from the verge of Heaven; eternal wrath
Burnt after them to the bottomless pit.
Hell heard the unsufferable noise: Hell saw
Heaven ruining from Heaven, and would have fled
Affrighted; but strict Fate had cast too deep
Her dark foundations, and too fast had bound.
Nine days they fell: confounded Chaos roared,
And felt tenfold confusion in their fall
Through his wild anarchy, so huge a rout
Incumbered him with ruin. Hell at last,
Yawning, received them whole, and on them closed:
Hell, their fit habitation, fraught with fire
Unquenchable, the house of woe and pain.
Disburdened Heaven rejoiced, and soon repaired
Her mural breach, returning whence it rolled.

(VI. 824-879,

The Messiah returns in triumph to the paternal throne, and is greeted with acclamations by the rejoicing myriads who remain in Heaven.

The first act in the great drama is finished.

'For the moment, therefore, there are three divisions of Universal Space, — HEAVEN, CHAOS, and HELL. Almost immediately, however, there is a fourth. Not only have the expelled Angels been nine days and nights in falling through Chaos to reach Hell; but, after they have reached Hell and it has closed over them, they lie for another period of nine days and nights (I. 50–53), stupefied and bewildered in the fiery gulf. It is during this second nine days that there takes place a great event, which farther modifies the map of Infinitude. Long had there been talk in Heaven of a new race of beings to be created at some time by the Almighty, inferior in some respects to the Angels, but in the history of whom, and of God's dealings with them, there was to be a display of the divine power and love which even the Angels might contemplate with wonder (VII. 139–183). The time for the creation of this new race of beings has now arrived. Scarcely have the Rebel Angels been enclosed in Hell, and Chaos has recovered from the turmoil of the descent of such a rout through its depths, when the Paternal Deity, addressing the Son, tells him that, in order to repair the loss caused to Heaven, the predetermined creation of Man and of the World of Man shall now take effect. It is for the Son to execute the will of the Father. Straightway he goes forth on his creating errand. The everlasting gates of Heaven open wide to let him pass forth; and, clothed with majesty, and accompanied with thousands of Seraphim and Cherubim, anxious to behold the great work to be done, he does pass forth — far into that very Chaos through which the Rebel Angels have so recently fallen, and which now intervenes between Heaven and Hell. At length he stays his fervid wheels, and, taking the golden compasses in his hands, centres one point of them where he stands, and turns the other through the obscure profundity around (VII. 224–231). Thus are marked out, or cut out, through the body of Chaos, the limits of the new Universe of Man, — that Starry Universe which to us seems measureless and the same as Infinity itself, but which is really only a beautiful azure sphere or drop, insolated in Chaos, and hung at its topmost point or zenith from the Empyrean. But, though the limits of the new experimental Creation are thus at once marked out, the completion of the Creation is a work of Six Days (VII. 242, 550). On the last of these, to crown the work, the happy Earth received its first human pair — the appointed lords of the entire new Creation. And so, resting from his labors, and beholding all that he had made, that it was good, the Messiah returned to his Father, reascending through the golden gates, which were now just over the zenith of the new World, and were its point of suspension from the Empyrean Heaven; and the Seventh Day or Sabbath was spent in songs of praise by all the Heavenly hosts over the finished work, and in contemplation of it as it hung beneath them,

> another Heaven,
> From Heaven-gate not far, founded in view
> On the clear hyaline.

And now, accordingly, this was the diagram of the Universal Infinitude:

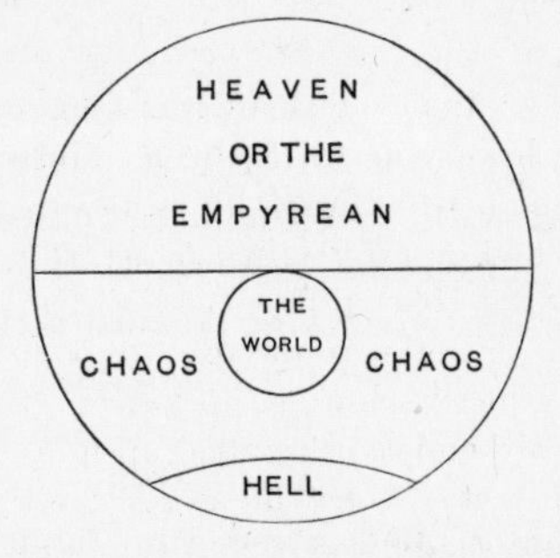

There are the three regions of HEAVEN, CHAOS, and HELL as before; but there is now also a fourth region, hung drop-like into Chaos by an attachment to Heaven at the north pole or zenith. This is the NEW WORLD, or the STARRY UNIVERSE,—all that Universe of orbs and galaxies which man's vision can reach by utmost power of telescope, and which even to his imagination is illimitable. And yet as to the proportions of this World to the total map Milton dares to be exact. The distance from its nadir or lowest point to the upper boss of Hell is exactly equal to its own radius: or, in other words, the distance of Hell-gate from

Heaven-gate is exactly three semidiameters of the Human or Starry Universe (I. 73, 74).' (Masson, *Introduction to Paradise Lost*, pp. 32–34.)

We have thus followed the events which make up the first part of the threefold story. We have been with Satan in that normal state of peace and innocence which he had shared for ages with the other Sons of God; in his first fault of rebellious pride; and in the overthrow of his overweening ambition. Before we proceed to the study of his character in its next stage of development, we may linger a moment over the first scene of that human life which has just begun, and which is to constitute a main, if not a paramount, interest throughout the rest of the poem.

'As new waked from soundest sleep,
Soft on the flowery herb I found me laid
In balmy sweat, which with his beams the Sun
Soon dried, and on the reeking moisture fed.
Straight toward Heaven my wondering eyes I turned,
And gazed awhile the ample sky, till, raised
By quick instinctive motion, up I sprung,
As thitherward endeavoring, and upright
Stood on my feet. About me round I saw
Hill, dale, and shady woods, and sunny plains,
And liquid lapse of murmuring streams: by these,
Creatures that lived and moved, and walked or flew;
Birds on the branches warbling: all things smiled;
With fragrance and with joy my heart o'erflowed.
Myself I then perused, and limb by limb
Surveyed, and sometimes went, and sometimes ran
With supple joints, as lively vigor led:
But who I was, or where, or from what cause,
Knew not. To speak I tried, and forthwith spake;
My tongue obeyed, and readily could name
Whate'er I saw. "Thou Sun," said I, "fair light,
And thou enlightened Earth, so fresh and gay;

Ye hills and dales, ye rivers, woods, and plains,
And ye that live and move, fair Creatures, tell,
Tell if ye saw, how came I thus? how here?
Not of myself; by some great Maker then,
In goodness and in power pre-eminent!
Tell me, how may I know him, how adore,
From whom I have that thus I move and live,
And feel that I am happier than I know!"
While thus I called, and strayed I knew not whither,
From where I first drew air, and first beheld
This happy light, when answer none returned,
On a green shady bank profuse of flowers,
Pensive I sat me down. There gentle sleep
First found me, and with soft oppression seized
My drowsed sense, untroubled.'

(VIII. 253–289.)

PARADISE LOST.

BOOK I.

The Printer to the Reader.

Courteous Reader, there was no Argument at first intended to the book; but for the satisfaction of many that have desired it, I have procured it, and withal a reason of that which stumbled many others, why the poem rimes not. — *S. Simmons.*

THE VERSE.

The measure is English heroic verse, without rime, as that of Homer in Greek, and of Virgil in Latin; rime being no necessary adjunct or true ornament of poem or good verse, in longer works especially, but the invention of a barbarous age, to set off wretched matter and lame metre; graced indeed since by the use of some famous modern poets, carried away by custom, but much to their own vexation, hindrance, and constraint to express many things otherwise, and for the most part worse, than else they would have expressed them. Not without cause, therefore, some both Italian and Spanish poets of prime note have rejected rime both in longer and shorter works, as have also, long since, our best English tragedies; as a thing of itself, to all judicious ears, trivial and of no true musical delight; which consists only in apt numbers, fit quantity of syllables, and the sense variously drawn out from one verse into another, not in the jingling sound of like endings, a fault avoided by the learned ancients both in poetry and all good oratory. This neglect then of rime so little is to be taken for a defect, though it may seem so perhaps to vulgar readers, that it rather is to be esteemed an example set, the first in English, of ancient liberty recovered to heroic poem from the troublesome and modern bondage of riming.

THE ARGUMENT.

THIS First Book proposes, first in brief, the whole subject: Man's disobedience, and the loss thereupon of Paradise, wherein he was placed: then touches the prime cause of his fall — the Serpent, or rather Satan in the Serpent; who, revolting from God, and drawing to his side many legions of Angels, was by the command of God driven out of Heaven with all his crew into the great Deep. Which action passed over, the Poem hastens into the midst of things; presenting Satan with his Angels now fallen into Hell — described here, not in the Centre (for heaven and earth may be supposed as yet not made, certainly not yet accursed), but in a place of utter darkness, fitliest called Chaos: here Satan with his Angels lying on the burning lake, thunderstruck and astonished, after a certain space recovers, as from confusion; calls up him who, next in order and dignity, lay by him; they confer of their miserable fall. Satan awakens all his legions, who lay till then in the same manner confounded. They rise: their numbers, array of battle, their chief leaders named, according to the idols known afterwards in Canaan and the countries adjoining. To these Satan directs his speech; comforts them with hope yet of regaining Heaven; but tells them lastly of a new world and new kind of creature to be created, according to an ancient prophecy or report in Heaven; for that Angels were long before this visible creation was the opinion of many ancient Fathers. To find out the truth of this prophecy, and what to determine thereon, he refers to a full council. What his associates thence attempt. Pandemonium, the palace of Satan, rises, suddenly built out of the Deep: the infernal Peers there sit in council.

PARADISE LOST.

BOOK I.

Of Man's first disobedience, and the fruit
Of that forbidden Tree, whose mortal taste
Brought death into the world, and all our woe,
With loss of Eden, till one greater Man
Restore us, and regain the blissful seat,
Sing, Heavenly Muse, that on the secret top
Of Oreb, or of Sinai, didst inspire
That shepherd who first taught the chosen seed
In the beginning how the Heavens and Earth
Rose out of Chaos: or, if Sion hill 10
Delight thee more, and Siloa's brook that flowed
Fast by the oracle of God, I thence
Invoke thy aid to my adventurous song,
That with no middle flight intends to soar
Above the Aonian mount, while it pursues
Things unattempted yet in prose or rhyme.
And chiefly Thou, O Spirit, that dost prefer
Before all temples the upright heart and pure,
Instruct me, for Thou know'st; Thou from the first
Wast present, and, with mighty wings outspread, 20
Dove-like sat'st brooding on the vast Abyss,
And madest it pregnant: what in me is dark
Illumine, what is low raise and support;
That to the highth of this great argument
I may assert Eternal Providence,
And justify the ways of God to men.

Say first — for Heaven hides nothing from Thy view,
Nor the deep tract of Hell — say first what cause
Moved our grand parents, in that happy state,
Favored of Heaven so highly, to fall off 30
From their Creator, and transgress his will
For one restraint, lords of the world besides.
Who first seduced them to that foul revolt?
The infernal Serpent; he it was, whose guile,
Stirred up with envy and revenge, deceived
The Mother of Mankind, what time his pride
Had cast him out from Heaven, with all his host
Of rebel Angels, by whose aid, aspiring
To set himself in glory above his peers,
He trusted to have equalled the Most High, 40
If he opposed; and with ambitious aim
Against the throne and monarchy of God
Raised impious war in Heaven, and battle proud,
With vain attempt. Him the Almighty Power
Hurled headlong flaming from the ethereal sky,
With hideous ruin and combustion, down
To bottomless perdition; there to dwell
In adamantine chains and penal fire,
Who durst defy the Omnipotent to arms.
Nine times the space that measures day and night 50
To mortal men, he with his horrid crew
Lay vanquished, rolling in the fiery gulf,
Confounded, though immortal. But his doom
Reserved him to more wrath; for now the thought
Both of lost happiness and lasting pain
Torments him; round he throws his baleful eyes,
That witnessed huge affliction and dismay,
Mixed with obdurate pride and steadfast hate.
At once, as far as Angels ken, he views
The dismal situation waste and wild: 60
A dungeon horrible on all sides round

As one great furnace flamed; yet from those flames
No light; but rather darkness visible
Served only to discover sights of woe,
Regions of sorrow, doleful shades, where peace
And rest can never dwell, hope never comes
That comes to all; but torture without end
Still urges, and a fiery deluge, fed
With ever-burning sulphur unconsumed.
Such place Eternal Justice had prepared 70
For those rebellious; here their prison ordained
In utter darkness, and their portion set,
As far removed from God and light of Heaven
As from the Centre thrice to the utmost pole.
Oh how unlike the place from whence they fell!
There the companions of his fall, o'erwhelmed
With floods and whirlwinds of tempestuous fire,
He soon discerns; and, weltering by his side,
One next himself in power, and next in crime,
Long after known in Palestine, and named 80
Beëlzebub. To whom the Arch-Enemy,
And thence in Heaven called *Satan*, with bold words
Breaking the horrid silence, thus began: —
'If thou beest he — but Oh how fallen! how changed
From him, — who in the happy realms of light,
Clothed with transcendent brightness, didst outshine
Myriads, though bright! if he whom mutual league,
United thoughts and counsels, equal hope
And hazard in the glorious enterprise,
Joined with me once, now misery hath joined 90
In equal ruin: into what pit thou seest
From what highth fallen; so much the stronger proved
He with his thunder: and till then who knew
The force of those dire arms? Yet not for those,
Nor what the potent Victor in his rage
Can else inflict, do I repent, or change,

Though changed in outward lustre, that fixed mind,
And high disdain from sense of injured merit,
That with the Mightiest raised me to contend,
And to the fierce contention brought along 100
Innumerable force of Spirits armed,
That durst dislike his reign, and, me preferring,
His utmost power with adverse power opposed
In dubious battle on the plains of Heaven,
And shook his throne. What though the field be lost?
All is not lost: the unconquerable will,
And study of revenge, immortal hate,
And courage never to submit or yield:
And what is else not to be overcome?
That glory never shall his wrath or might 110
Extort from me. To bow and sue for grace
With suppliant knee, and deify his power
Who, from the terror of this arm, so late
Doubted his empire — that were low indeed;
That were an ignominy and shame beneath
This downfall; since by fate the strength of gods
And this empyreal substance cannot fail;
Since, through experience of this great event,
In arms not worse, in foresight much advanced,
We may with more successful hope resolve 120
To wage by force or guile eternal war,
Irreconcilable to our grand foe,
Who now triumphs, and in the excess of joy
Sole reigning holds the tyranny of Heaven.'

So spake the apostate Angel, though in pain,
Vaunting aloud, but racked with deep despair;
And him thus answered soon his bold compeer: —

'O Prince! O Chief of many throned Powers!
That led the embattled Seraphim to war
Under thy conduct, and, in dreadful deeds 130
Fearless, endangered Heaven's perpetual King,

And put to proof his high supremacy,
Whether upheld by strength, or chance, or fate!
Too well I see and rue the dire event
That with sad overthrow and foul defeat
Hath lost us Heaven, and all this mighty host
In horrible destruction laid thus low,
As far as gods and Heavenly essences
Can perish: for the mind and spirit remains
Invincible, and vigor soon returns, 140
Though all our glory extinct, and happy state
Here swallowed up in endless misery.
But what if he our Conqueror (whom I now
Of force believe almighty, since no less
Than such could have o'erpowered such force as ours)
Have left us this our spirit and strength entire,
Strongly to suffer and support our pains,
That we may so suffice his vengeful ire;
Or do him mightier service, as his thralls
By right of war, whate'er his business be, 150
Here in the heart of Hell to work in fire,
Or do his errands in the gloomy Deep?
What can it then avail, though yet we feel
Strength undiminished, or eternal being
To undergo eternal punishment?'
Whereto with speedy words the Arch-Fiend replied:—
'Fallen Cherub, to be weak is miserable,
Doing or suffering: but of this be sure—
To do aught good never will be our task,
But ever to do ill our sole delight, 160
As being the contrary to his high will
Whom we resist. If then his providence
Out of our evil seek to bring forth good,
Our labor must be to pervert that end,
And out of good still to find means of evil;
Which ofttimes may succeed, so as perhaps

Shall grieve him, if I fail not, and disturb
His inmost counsels from their destined aim.
But see! the angry Victor hath recalled
His ministers of vengeance and pursuit 170
Back to the gates of Heaven; the sulphurous hail,
Shot after us in storm, o'erblown hath laid
The fiery surge that from the precipice
Of Heaven received us falling; and the thunder,
Winged with red lightning and impetuous rage,
Perhaps hath spent his shafts, and ceases now
To bellow through the vast and boundless Deep.
Let us not slip the occasion, whether scorn
Or satiate fury yield it from our foe.
Seest thou yon dreary plain, forlorn and wild, 180
The seat of desolation, void of light,
Save what the glimmering of these livid flames
Casts pale and dreadful? Thither let us tend
From off the tossing of these fiery waves;
There rest, if any rest can harbor there;
And, reassembling our afflicted powers,
Consult how we may henceforth most offend
Our Enemy, our own loss how repair,
How overcome this dire calamity,
What reinforcement we may gain from hope, 190
If not what resolution from despair.'
 Thus Satan, talking to his nearest mate,
With head uplift above the wave, and eyes
That sparkling blazed; his other parts besides,
Prone on the flood, extended long and large,
Lay floating many a rood, in bulk as huge
As whom the fables name of monstrous size,
Titanian, or Earth-born, that warred on Jove,
Briareos or Typhon, whom the den
By ancient Tarsus held, or that sea-beast 200
Leviathan, which God of all his works

Created hugest that swim the ocean-stream.
Him, haply, slumbering on the Norway foam,
The pilot of some small night-foundered skiff
Deeming some island, oft, as seamen tell,
With fixed anchor in his scaly rind,
Moors by his side under the lee, while night
Invests the sea, and wished morn delays.
So stretched out huge in length the Arch-Fiend lay,
Chained on the burning lake; nor ever thence 210
Had risen or heaved his head, but that the will
And high permission of all-ruling Heaven
Left him at large to his own dark designs,
That with reiterated crimes he might
Heap on himself damnation, while he sought
Evil to others, and enraged might see
How all his malice served but to bring forth
Infinite goodness, grace, and mercy, shewn
On Man by him seduced; but on himself
Treble confusion, wrath, and vengeance poured. 220
Forthwith upright he rears from off the pool
His mighty stature; on each hand the flames
Driven backward slope their pointing spires, and, rolled
In billows, leave in the midst a horrid vale.
Then with expanded wings he steers his flight
Aloft, incumbent on the dusky air,
That felt unusual weight; till on dry land
He lights — if it were land that ever burned
With solid, as the lake with liquid fire,
And such appeared in hue, as when the force 230
Of subterranean wind transports a hill
Torn from Pelorus, or the shattered side
Of thundering Ætna, whose combustible
And fuelled entrails thence conceiving fire,
Sublimed with mineral fury, aid the winds,
And leave a singed bottom all involved

With stench and smoke: such resting found the sole
Of unblest feet. Him followed his next mate,
Both glorying to have scaped the Stygian flood
As gods, and by their own recovered strength, 240
Not by the sufferance of supernal power.
'Is this the region, this the soil, the clime,'
Said then the lost Archangel, 'this the seat
That we must change for Heaven? this mournful gloom
For that celestial light? Be it so, since he
Who now is sovran can dispose and bid
What shall be right: farthest from him is best,
Whom reason hath equalled, force hath made supreme
Above his equals. Farewell, happy fields,
Where joy forever dwells! Hail, horrors! hail, 250
Infernal world! and thou, profoundest Hell,
Receive thy new possessor, one who brings
A mind not to be changed by place or time.
The mind is its own place, and in itself
Can make a Heaven of Hell, a Hell of Heaven.
What matter where, if I be still the same,
And what I should be, all but less than he
Whom thunder hath made greater? Here at least
We shall be free; the Almighty hath not built
Here for his envy, will not drive us hence: 260
Here we may reign secure, and in my choice
To reign is worth ambition, though in Hell:
Better to reign in Hell, than serve in Heaven.
But wherefore let we then our faithful friends,
The associates and co-partners of our loss,
Lie thus astonished on the oblivious pool,
And call them not to share with us their part
In this unhappy mansion, or once more
With rallied arms to try what may be yet
Regained in Heaven, or what more lost in Hell?' 270
So Satan spake; and him Beëlzebub

Thus answered: — 'Leader of those armies bright
Which but the Omnipotent none could have foiled,
If once they hear that voice, their liveliest pledge
Of hope in fears and dangers — heard so oft
In worst extremes, and on the perilous edge
Of battle when it raged, in all assaults
Their surest signal — they will soon resume
New courage and revive, though now they lie
Grovelling and prostrate on yon lake of fire, 280
As we erewhile, astounded and amazed:
No wonder, fallen such a pernicious highth!'
He scarce had ceased when the superior Fiend
Was moving toward the shore; his ponderous shield,
Ethereal temper, massy, large, and round,
Behind him cast. The broad circumference
Hung on his shoulders like the moon, whose orb
Through optic glass the Tuscan artist views
At evening from the top of Fesole,
Or in Valdarno, to descry new lands, 290
Rivers, or mountains, in her spotty globe.
His spear — to equal which the tallest pine
Hewn on Norwegian hills, to be the mast
Of some great ammiral, were but a wand —
He walked with, to support uneasy steps
Over the burning marle, not like those steps
On Heaven's azure; and the torrid clime
Smote on him sore besides, vaulted with fire.
Nathless he so endured, till on the beach
Of that inflamed sea he stood, and called 300
His legions, Angel forms, who lay entranced,
Thick as autumnal leaves that strow the brooks
In Vallombrosa, where the Etrurian shades
High over-arched embower; or scattered sedge
Afloat, when with fierce winds Orion armed
Hath vexed the Red-Sea coast, whose waves o'erthrew

Busiris and his Memphian chivalry,
While with perfidious hatred they pursued
The sojourners of Goshen, who beheld
From the safe shore their floating carcases 310
And broken chariot-wheels: so thick bestrown,
Abject and lost, lay these, covering the flood,
Under amazement of their hideous change.
He called so loud that all the hollow deep
Of Hell resounded:—'Princes, Potentates,
Warriors! the Flower of Heaven, once yours; now lost,
If such astonishment as this can seize
Eternal Spirits! Or have ye chosen this place
After the toil of battle to repose
Your wearied virtue, for the ease you find 320
To slumber here, as in the vales of Heaven?
Or in this abject posture have ye sworn
To adore the Conqueror, who now beholds
Cherub and Seraph rolling in the flood
With scattered arms and ensigns, till anon
His swift pursuers from Heaven-gates discern
The advantage, and descending tread us down
Thus drooping, or with linked thunderbolts
Transfix us to the bottom of this gulf?
Awake, arise, or be forever fallen!' 330
They heard, and were abashed, and up they sprung
Upon the wing, as when men wont to watch,
On duty sleeping found by whom they dread,
Rouse and bestir themselves ere well awake.
Nor did they not perceive the evil plight
In which they were, or the fierce pains not feel;
Yet to their General's voice they soon obeyed
Innumerable. As when the potent rod
Of Amram's son, in Egypt's evil day,
Waved round the coast, up called a pitchy cloud 340
Of locusts, warping on the eastern wind,

That o'er the realm of impious Pharaoh hung
Like night, and darkened all the land of Nile:
So numberless were those bad Angels seen
Hovering on wing under the cope of Hell,
'Twixt upper, nether, and surrounding fires;
Till, as a signal given, the uplifted spear
Of their great Sultan waving to direct
Their course, in even balance down they light
On the firm brimstone, and fill all the plain: 350
A multitude like which the populous North
Poured never from her frozen loins, to pass
Rhene or the Danaw, when her barbarous sons
Came like a deluge on the South, and spread
Beneath Gibraltar to the Libyan sands.
Forthwith, from every squadron and each band,
The heads and leaders thither haste where stood
Their great Commander; godlike shapes, and forms
Excelling human, princely Dignities,
And Powers that erst in Heaven sat on thrones; 360
Though of their names in Heavenly records now
Be no memorial, blotted out and rased
By their rebellion from the Books of Life.
Nor had they yet among the sons of Eve
Got them new names, till, wandering o'er the Earth,
Through God's high sufferance for the trial of man,
By falsities and lies the greatest part
Of mankind they corrupted to forsake
God their Creator; and the invisible
Glory of him that made them, to transform 370
Oft to the image of a brute, adorned
With gay religions full of pomp and gold,
And devils to adore for deities:
Then were they known to men by various names,
And various idols through the heathen world.
 Say, Muse, their names then known, who first, who last,

Roused from the slumber on that fiery couch,
At their great Emperor's call, as next in worth
Came singly where he stood on the bare strand,
While the promiscuous crowd stood yet aloof. 380
The chief were those who, from the pit of Hell
Roaming to seek their prey on Earth, durst fix
Their seats long after next the seat of God,
Their altars by his altar, gods adored
Among the nations round, and durst abide
Jehovah thundering out of Sion, throned
Between the Cherubim; yea, often placed
Within his sanctuary itself their shrines,
Abominations; and with cursed things
His holy rites and solemn feasts profaned, 390
And with their darkness durst affront his light.
First *Moloch*, horrid king, besmeared with blood
Of human sacrifice, and parents' tears,
Though, for the noise of drums and timbrels loud,
Their children's cries unheard that passed through fire
To his grim idol. Him the Ammonite
Worshiped in Rabba and her watery plain,
In Argob and in Basan, to the stream
Of utmost Arnon. Nor content with such
Audacious neighborhood, the wisest heart 400
Of Solomon he led by fraud to build
His temple right against the temple of God
On that opprobrious hill, and made his grove
The pleasant valley of Hinnom, Tophet thence
And black Gehenna called, the type of Hell.
Next *Chemos*, the obscene dread of Moab's sons,
From Aroar to Nebo, and the wild
Of southmost Abarim; in Hesebon
And Horonaim, Seon's realm, beyond
The flowery dale of Sibma clad with vines, 410
And Elealè to the Asphaltic pool.

Peor his other name, when he enticed
Israel in Sittim, on their march from Nile,
To do him wanton rites, which cost them woe.
Yet thence his lustful orgies he enlarged
Even to that hill of scandal, by the grove
Of Moloch homicide, lust hard by hate;
Till good Josiah drove them thence to Hell.
With these came they who, from the bordering flood
Of old Euphrates to the brook that parts 420
Egypt from Syrian ground, had general names
Of *Baalim* and *Ashtaroth* — those male,
These feminine. For Spirits, when they please,
Can either sex assume, or both; so soft
And uncompounded is their essence pure,
Not tied or manacled with joint or limb,
Nor founded on the brittle strength of bones,
Like cumbrous flesh; but, in what shape they choose,
Dilated or condensed, bright or obscure,
Can execute their aery purposes, 430
And works of love or enmity fulfil.
For those the race of Israel oft forsook
Their living Strength, and unfrequented left
His righteous altar, bowing lowly down
To bestial gods; for which their heads as low
Bowed down in battle, sunk before the spear
Of despicable foes. With these in troop
Came *Astoreth*, whom the Phœnicians called
Astarte, Queen of Heaven, with crescent horns;
To whose bright image nightly by the moon 440
Sidonian virgins paid their vows and songs;
In Sion also not unsung, where stood
Her temple on the offensive mountain, built
By that uxorious king whose heart, though large,
Beguiled by fair idolatresses, fell
To idols foul. *Thammuz* came next behind,

Whose annual wound in Lebanon allured
The Syrian damsels to lament his fate
In amorous ditties all a summer's day,
While smooth Adonis from his native rock 450
Ran purple to the sea, supposed with blood
Of Thammuz yearly wounded: the love-tale
Infected Sion's daughters with like heat,
Whose wanton passions in the sacred porch
Ezekiel saw, when, by the vision led,
His eye surveyed the dark idolatries
Of alienated Judah. Next came one
Who mourned in earnest, when the captive ark
Maimed his brute image, head and hands lopt off
In his own temple, on the grunsel-edge, 460
Where he fell flat, and shamed his worshipers:
Dagon his name, sea-monster, upward man
And downward fish; yet had his temple high
Reared in Azotus, dreaded through the coast
Of Palestine, in Gath and Ascalon,
And Accaron and Gaza's frontier bounds.
Him followed *Rimmon*, whose delightful seat
Was fair Damascus, on the fertile banks
Of Abbana and Pharphar, lucid streams.
He also against the house of God was bold: 470
A leper once he lost, and gained a king,
Ahaz, his sottish conqueror, whom he drew
God's altar to disparage and displace
For one of Syrian mode, whereon to burn
His odious offerings, and adore the gods
Whom he had vanquished. After these appeared
A crew who, under names of old renown,
Osiris, Isis, Orus, and their train,
With monstrous shapes and sorceries abused
Fanatic Egypt and her priests, to seek 480
Their wandering gods disguised in brutish forms

Rather than human. Nor did Israel scape
The infection, when their borrowed gold composed
The calf in Oreb; and the rebel king
Doubled that sin in Bethel and in Dan,
Likening his Maker to the grazed ox—
Jehovah, who, in one night, when he passed
From Egypt marching, equalled with one stroke
Both her first-born and all her bleating gods.
Belial came last, than whom a Spirit more lewd 490
Fell not from Heaven, or more gross to love
Vice for itself. To him no temple stood
Or altar smoked; yet who more oft than he
In temples and at altars, when the priest
Turns atheist, as did Eli's sons, who filled
With lust and violence the house of God?
In courts and palaces he also reigns,
And in luxurious cities, where the noise
Of riot ascends above their loftiest towers,
And injury and outrage; and when night 500
Darkens the streets, then wander forth the sons
Of Belial, flown with insolence and wine.
Witness the streets of Sodom, and that night
In Gibeah, when the hospitable door
Exposed a matron, to avoid worse rape.
These were the prime in order and in might;
The rest were long to tell; though far renowned
The Ionian gods—of Javan's issue held
Gods, yet confessed later than Heaven and Earth,
Their boasted parents—*Titan*, Heaven's first-born, 510
With his enormous brood, and birthright seized
By younger *Saturn;* he from mightier *Jove*,
His own and Rhea's son, like measure found;
So Jove usurping reigned. These, first in Crete
And Ida known, thence on the snowy top
Of cold Olympus ruled the middle air,

Their highest Heaven; or on the Delphian cliff,
Or in Dodona, and through all the bounds
Of Doric land; or who with Saturn old
Fled over Adria to the Hesperian fields, 520
And o'er the Celtic roamed the utmost isles.
All these and more came flocking; but with looks
Downcast and damp, yet such wherein appeared
Obscure some glimpse of joy, to have found their Chief
Not in despair, to have found themselves not lost
In loss itself; which on his countenance cast
Like doubtful hue. But he, his wonted pride
Soon recollecting, with high words that bore
Semblance of worth, not substance, gently raised
Their fainting courage, and dispelled their fears: 530
Then straight commands that at the warlike sound
Of trumpets loud and clarions, be upreared
His mighty standard. That proud honor claimed
Azazel as his right, a Cherub tall:
Who forthwith from the glittering staff unfurled
The imperial ensign, which, full high advanced,
Shone like a meteor streaming to the wind,
With gems and golden lustre rich emblazed,
Seraphic arms and trophies; all the while
Sonorous metal blowing martial sounds: 540
At which the universal host up-sent
A shout that tore Hell's concave, and beyond
Frighted the reign of Chaos and old Night.
All in a moment through the gloom were seen
Ten thousand banners rise into the air,
With orient colors waving; with them rose
A forest huge of spears; and thronging helms
Appeared, and serried shields in thick array
Of depth immeasurable. Anon they move
In perfect phalanx to the Dorian mood 550
Of flutes and soft recorders — such as raised

To highth of noblest temper heroes old
Arming to battle, and instead of rage
Deliberate valor breathed, firm and unmoved
With dread of death to flight or foul retreat;
Nor wanting power to mitigate and swage
With solemn touches troubled thoughts, and chase
Anguish and doubt and fear and sorrow and pain
From mortal or immortal minds. Thus they,
Breathing united force with fixed thought, 560
Moved on in silence to soft pipes that charmed
Their painful steps o'er the burnt soil; and now
Advanced in view they stand, a horrid front
Of dreadful length and dazzling arms, in guise
Of warriors old, with ordered spear and shield,
Awaiting what command their mighty chief
Had to impose. He through the armed files
Darts his experienced eye, and soon traverse
The whole battalion views — their order due,
Their visages and stature as of gods; 570
Their number last he sums. And now his heart
Distends with pride, and hardening in his strength
Glories; for never, since created man,
Met such embodied force as, named with these,
Could merit more than that small infantry
Warred on by cranes: though all the giant brood
Of Phlegra with the heroic race were joined
That fought at Thebes and Ilium, on each side
Mixed with auxiliar gods; and what resounds
In fable or romance of Uther's son, 580
Begirt with British and Armoric knights;
And all who since, baptized or infidel,
Jousted in Aspramont, or Montalban,
Damasco, or Marocco, or Trebisond;
Or whom Biserta sent from Afric shore
When Charlemain with all his peerage fell

By Fontarabbia. Thus far these beyond
Compare of mortal prowess, yet observed
Their dread commander. He, above the rest
In shape and gesture proudly eminent, 590
Stood like a tower; his form had yet not lost
All her original brightness, nor appeared
Less than Archangel ruined, and the excess
Of glory obscured: as when the sun new-risen
Looks through the horizontal misty air
Shorn of his beams, or from behind the moon,
In dim eclipse, disastrous twilight sheds
On half the nations, and with fear of change
Perplexes monarchs. Darkened so, yet shone
Above them all the Archangel: but his face 600
Deep scars of thunder had intrenched, and care
Sat on his faded cheek, but under brows
Of dauntless courage, and considerate pride
Waiting revenge. Cruel his eye, but cast
Signs of remorse and passion, to behold
The fellows of his crime, the followers rather
(Far other once beheld in bliss), condemned
Forever now to have their lot in pain;
Millions of Spirits for his fault amerced
Of Heaven, and from eternal splendors flung 610
For his revolt; yet faithful how they stood,
Their glory withered: as, when Heaven's fire
Hath scathed the forest oaks or mountain pines,
With singed top their stately growth, though bare,
Stands on the blasted heath. He now prepared
To speak; whereat their doubled ranks they bend
From wing to wing, and half enclose him round
With all his peers: attention held them mute.
Thrice he assayed, and thrice, in spite of scorn,
Tears, such as Angels weep, burst forth: at last 620
Words interwove with sighs found out their way: —

'O myriads of immortal Spirits! O Powers
Matchless, but with the Almighty!—and that strife
Was not inglorious, though the event was dire,
As this place testifies, and this dire change,
Hateful to utter. But what power of mind,
Foreseeing or presaging, from the depth
Of knowledge past or present, could have feared
How such united force of gods, how such
As stood like these, could ever know repulse? 630
For who can yet believe, though after loss,
That all these puissant legions, whose exile
Hath emptied Heaven, shall fail to reascend,
Self-raised, and repossess their native seat?
For me, be witness all the host of Heaven,
If counsels different, or dangers shunned
By me, have lost our hopes. But he who reigns
Monarch in Heaven, till then as one secure
Sat on his throne, upheld by old repute,
Consent or custom, and his regal state 640
Put forth at full, but still his strength concealed;
Which tempted our attempt, and wrought our fall.
Henceforth his might we know, and know our own,
So as not either to provoke, or dread
New war provoked. Our better part remains
To work in close design, by fraud or guile,
What force effected not; that he no less
At length from us may find, Who overcomes
By force hath overcome but half his foe.
Space may produce new worlds; whereof so rife 650
There went a fame in Heaven that He erelong
Intended to create, and therein plant
A generation whom his choice regard
Should favor equal to the Sons of Heaven.
Thither, if but to pry, shall be perhaps
Our first eruption: thither or elsewhere;

For this infernal pit shall never hold
Celestial Spirits in bondage, nor the Abyss
Long under darkness cover. But these thoughts
Full counsel must mature. Peace is despaired, 660
For who can think submission? War, then, war
Open or understood, must be resolved.'
He spake; and, to confirm his words, out-flew
Millions of flaming swords, drawn from the thighs
Of mighty Cherubim; the sudden blaze
Far round illumined Hell. Highly they raged
Against the Highest, and fierce with grasped arms
Clashed on their sounding shields the din of war,
Hurling defiance toward the vault of Heaven.
There stood a hill not far, whose grisly top 670
Belched fire and rolling smoke; the rest entire
Shone with a glossy scurf, undoubted sign
That in his womb was hid metallic ore,
The work of sulphur. Thither, winged with speed,
A numerous brigad hastened: as when bands
Of pioners, with spade and pickaxe armed,
Forerun the royal camp, to trench a field,
Or cast a rampart. Mammon led them on,
Mammon, the least erected Spirit that fell 679
From Heaven, for even in Heaven his looks and thoughts
Were always downward bent, admiring more
The riches of Heaven's pavement, trodden gold,
Than aught divine or holy else enjoyed
In vision beatific. By him first
Men also, and by his suggestion taught,
Ransacked the Centre, and with impious hands
Rifled the bowels of their mother Earth
For treasures better hid. Soon had his crew
Opened into the hill a spacious wound,
And digged out ribs of gold. Let none admire 690
That riches grow in Hell; that soil may best

Deserve the precious bane. And here let those
Who boast in mortal things, and wondering tell
Of Babel, and the works of Memphian kings,
Learn how their greatest monuments of fame,
And strength, and art, are easily outdone
By Spirits reprobate, and in an hour
What in an age they, with incessant toil
And hands innumerable, scarce perform.
Nigh on the plain, in many cells prepared, 700
That underneath had veins of liquid fire
Sluiced from the lake, a second multitude
With wondrous art founded the massy ore,
Severing each kind, and scummed the bullion-dross.
A third as soon had formed within the ground
A various mould, and from the boiling cells
By strange conveyance filled each hollow nook:
As in an organ, from one blast of wind,
To many a row of pipes the sound-board breathes.
Anon out of the earth a fabric huge 710
Rose like an exhalation, with the sound
Of dulcet symphonies and voices sweet—
Built like a temple, where pilasters round
Were set, and Doric pillars overlaid
With golden architrave; nor did there want
Cornice or frieze, with bossy sculptures graven:
The roof was fretted gold. Not Babylon,
Nor great Alcairo, such magnificence
Equalled in all their glories, to enshrine
Belus or Serapis their gods, or seat 720
Their kings, when Egypt with Assyria strove
In wealth and luxury. The ascending pile
Stood fixed her stately highth, and straight the doors,
Opening their brazen folds, discover, wide
Within, her ample spaces o'er the smooth
And level pavement: from the arched roof,

Pendent by subtle magic, many a row
Of starry lamps and blazing cressets, fed
With naphtha and asphaltus, yielded light
As from a sky. The hasty multitude 730
Admiring entered, and the work some praise,
And some the architect. His hand was known
In Heaven by many a towered structure high,
Where sceptred Angels held their residence,
And sat as Princes, whom the supreme King
Exalted to such power, and gave to rule,
Each in his Hierarchy, the Orders bright.
Nor was his name unheard or unadored
In ancient Greece; and in Ausonian land
Men called him Mulciber; and how he fell 740
From Heaven they fabled, thrown by angry Jove
Sheer o'er the crystal battlements: from morn
To noon he fell, from noon to dewy eve,
A summer's day; and with the setting sun
Dropt from the zenith, like a falling star,
On Lemnos, the Ægæan isle. Thus they relate,
Erring; for he with this rebellious rout
Fell long before; nor aught availed him now
To have built in Heaven high towers; nor did he scape
By all his engines, but was headlong sent 750
With his industrious crew to build in Hell.
Meanwhile the winged haralds, by command
Of sovran power, with awful ceremony
And trumpet's sound, throughout the host proclaim
A solemn council forthwith to be held
At Pandemonium, the high capital
Of Satan and his peers. Their summons called
From every band and squared regiment
By place or choice the worthiest; they anon
With hundreds and with thousands trooping came 760
Attended. All access was thronged, the gates
And porches wide, but chief the spacious hall

(Though like a covered field, where champions bold
Wont ride in armed, and at the Soldan's chair
Defied the best of Panim chivalry
To mortal combat, or career with lance)
Thick swarmed, both on the ground and in the air,
Brushed with the hiss of rustling wings. As bees
In spring-time, when the Sun with Taurus rides,
Pour forth their populous youth about the hive 770
In clusters; they among fresh dews and flowers
Fly to and fro, or on the smoothed plank,
The suburb of their straw-built citadel,
New rubbed with balm, expatiate and confer
Their state-affairs. So thick the aery crowd
Swarmed and were straightened; till, the signal given,
Behold a wonder! they but now who seemed
In bigness to surpass Earth's giant sons,
Now less than smallest dwarfs, in narrow room
Throng numberless, like that pygmean race 780
Beyond the Indian mount; or faery elves,
Whose midnight revels, by a forest-side
Or fountain, some belated peasant sees,
Or dreams he sees, while overhead the Moon
Sits arbitress, and nearer to the Earth
Wheels her pale course; they, on their mirth and dance
Intent, with jocund music charm his ear;
At once with joy and fear his heart rebounds.
Thus incorporeal Spirits to smallest forms
Reduced their shapes immense, and were at large, 790
Though without number still, amidst the hall
Of that infernal court. But far within,
And in their own dimensions like themselves,
The great Seraphic Lords and Cherubim
In close recess and secret conclave sat,
A thousand demi-gods on golden seats,
Frequent and full. After short silence then,
And summons read, the great consult began.

PARADISE LOST.

BOOK II.

THE ARGUMENT.

THE consultation begun, Satan debates whether another battle be to be hazarded for the recovery of Heaven: some advise it, others dissuade. A third proposal is preferred, mentioned before by Satan, to search the truth of that prophecy or tradition in Heaven concerning another world, and another kind of creature, equal, or not much inferior, to themselves, about this time to be created. Their doubt who shall be sent on this difficult search: Satan, their chief, undertakes alone the voyage; is honored and applauded. The council thus ended, the rest betake them several ways and to several employments, as their inclinations lead them, to entertain the time till Satan return. He passes on his journey to Hell-gates, finds them shut, and who sat there to guard them; by whom at length they are opened, and discover to him the great gulf between Hell and Heaven; with what difficulty he passes through, directed by Chaos, the Power of that place, to the sight of this new World which he sought.

PARADISE LOST.

BOOK II.

High on a throne of royal state, which far
Outshone the wealth of Ormus and of Ind,
Or where the gorgeous East with richest hand
Showers on her kings barbaric pearl and gold,
Satan exalted sat, by merit raised
To that bad eminence; and, from despair
Thus high uplifted beyond hope, aspires
Beyond thus high, insatiate to pursue
Vain war with Heaven; and, by success untaught,
His proud imaginations thus displayed:— 10
'Powers and Dominions, Deities of Heaven!
For since no deep within her gulf can hold
Immortal vigor, though oppressed and fallen,
I give not Heaven for lost: from this descent
Celestial Virtues rising will appear
More glorious and more dread than from no fall,
And trust themselves to fear no second fate.
Me though just right, and the fixed laws of Heaven,
Did first create your leader, next, free choice,
With what besides, in counsel or in fight, 20
Hath been achieved of merit, yet this loss,
Thus far at least recovered, hath much more
Established in a safe unenvied throne,
Yielded with full consent. The happier state
In Heaven, which follows dignity, might draw
Envy from each inferior; but who here

Will envy whom the highest place exposes
Foremost to stand against the Thunderer's aim
Your bulwark, and condemns to greatest share
Of endless pain? Where there is then no good 30
For which to strive, no strife can grow up there
From faction; for none sure will claim in Hell
Precedence, none whose portion is so small
Of present pain that with ambitious mind
Will covet more. With this advantage then
To union, and firm faith, and firm accord,
More than can be in Heaven, we now return
To claim our just inheritance of old,
Surer to prosper than prosperity
Could have assured us; and by what best way, 40
Whether of open war or covert guile,
We now debate; who can advise may speak.'

He ceased; and next him Moloch, sceptred king,
Stood up, the strongest and the fiercest Spirit
That fought in Heaven, now fiercer by despair.
His trust was with the Eternal to be deemed
Equal in strength, and rather than be less
Cared not to be at all; with that care lost
Went all his fear: of God, or Hell, or worse,
He recked not, and these words thereafter spake:— 50

'My sentence is for open war. Of wiles,
More unexpert, I boast not: them let those
Contrive who need, or when they need; not now.
For while they sit contriving, shall the rest—
Millions that stand in arms, and longing wait
The signal to ascend—sit lingering here,
Heaven's fugitives, and for their dwelling-place
Accept this dark opprobrious den of shame,
The prison of his tyranny who reigns
By our delay? No! let us rather choose, 60
Armed with Hell-flames and fury, all at once

O'er Heaven's high towers to force resistless way,
Turning our tortures into horrid arms
Against the Torturer; when to meet the noise
Of his almighty engine he shall hear
Infernal thunder, and for lightning see
Black fire and horror shot with equal rage
Among his Angels, and his throne itself
Mixed with Tartarean sulphur and strange fire,
His own invented torments. But perhaps 70
The way seems difficult and steep to scale
With upright wing against a higher foe.
Let such bethink them, if the sleepy drench
Of that forgetful lake benumb not still,
That in our proper motion we ascend
Up to our native seat; descent and fall
To us is adverse. Who but felt of late,
When the fierce foe hung on our broken rear
Insulting, and pursued us through the deep,
With what compulsion and laborious flight 80
We sunk thus low? The ascent is easy then.
The event is feared: should we again provoke
Our stronger, some worse way his wrath may find
To our destruction—if there be in Hell
Fear to be worse destroyed! What can be worse
Than to dwell here, driven out from bliss, condemned
In this abhorred deep to utter woe;
Where pain of unextinguishable fire
Must exercise us, without hope of end,
The vassals of his anger, when the scourge 90
Inexorably, and the torturing hour,
Calls us to penance? More destroyed than thus,
We should be quite abolished, and expire.
What fear we then? what doubt we to incense
His utmost ire? which, to the highth enraged,
Will either quite consume us, and reduce

To nothing this essential — happier far
Than miserable to have eternal being! —
Or if our substance be indeed divine,
And cannot cease to be, we are at worst 100
On this side nothing; and by proof we feel
Our power sufficient to disturb his Heaven,
And with perpetual inroads to alarm,
Though inaccessible, his fatal throne:
Which, if not victory, is yet revenge.'
He ended frowning, and his look denounced
Desperate revenge, and battle dangerous
To less than gods. On the other side up rose
Belial, in act more graceful and humane;
A fairer person lost not Heaven; he seemed 110
For dignity composed, and high exploit.
But all was false and hollow; though his tongue
Dropt manna, and could make the worse appear
The better reason, to perplex and dash
Maturest counsels: for his thoughts were low;
To vice industrious, but to nobler deeds
Timorous and slothful; yet he pleased the ear:
And with persuasive accent thus began: —
'I should be much for open war, O Peers,
As not behind in hate, if what was urged 120
Main reason to persuade immediate war
Did not dissuade me most, and seem to cast
Ominous conjecture on the whole success;
When he who most excels in fact of arms,
In what he counsels and in what excels
Mistrustful, grounds his courage on despair
And utter dissolution, as the scope
Of all his aim, after some dire revenge.
First, what revenge? The towers of Heaven are filled
With armed watch, that render all access 130
Impregnable: oft on the bordering deep

Encamp their legions, or with obscure wing
Scout far and wide into the realm of Night,
Scorning surprise. Or could we break our way
By force, and at our heels all Hell should rise
With blackest insurrection, to confound
Heaven's purest light, yet our great Enemy,
All incorruptible, would on his throne
Sit unpolluted, and the ethereal mould,
Incapable of stain, would soon expel 140
Her mischief, and purge off the baser fire,
Victorious. Thus repulsed, our final hope
Is flat despair: we must exasperate
The Almighty Victor to spend all his rage;
And that must end us, that must be our cure—
To be no more. Sad cure! for who would lose,
Though full of pain, this intellectual being,
Those thoughts that wander through eternity,
To perish rather, swallowed up and lost
In the wide womb of uncreated Night, 150
Devoid of sense and motion? And who knows,
Let this be good, whether our angry foe
Can give it, or will ever? How he can
Is doubtful; that he never will is sure.
Will he, so wise, let loose at once his ire,
Belike through impotence, or unaware,
To give his enemies their wish, and end
Them in his anger, whom his anger saves
To punish endless? "Wherefore cease we, then?"
Say they who counsel war; "we are decreed, 160
Reserved, and destined to eternal woe;
Whatever doing, what can we suffer more,
What can we suffer worse?" Is this then worst
Thus sitting, thus consulting, thus in arms?
What when we fled amain, pursued and strook
With Heaven's afflicting thunder, and besought

The Deep to shelter us? this Hell then seemed
A refuge from those wounds. Or when we lay
Chained on the burning lake? that sure was worse.
What if the breath that kindled those grim fires, 170
Awaked, should blow them into sevenfold rage,
And plunge us in the flames? or from above
Should intermitted vengeance arm again
His red right hand to plague us? What if all
Her stores were opened, and this firmament
Of Hell should spout her cataracts of fire,
Impendent horrors, threatening hideous fall
One day upon our heads; while we perhaps,
Designing or exhorting glorious war,
Caught in a fiery tempest, shall be hurled, 180
Each on his rock transfixed, the sport and prey
Of racking whirlwinds, or forever sunk
Under yon boiling ocean, wrapt in chains;
There to converse with everlasting groans,
Unrespited, unpitied, unreprieved,
Ages of hopeless end! This would be worse.
War therefore, open or concealed, alike
My voice dissuades; for what can force or guile
With him, or who deceive his mind, whose eye
Views all things at one view? He from Heaven's highth
All these our motions vain sees and derides; 191
Not more almighty to resist our might
Than wise to frustrate all our plots and wiles.
Shall we then live thus vile, the race of Heaven
Thus trampled, thus expelled to suffer here
Chains and these torments? Better these than worse,
By my advice; since fate inevitable
Subdues us, and omnipotent decree,
The Victor's will. To suffer, as to do,
Our strength is equal, nor the law unjust 200
That so ordains: this was at first resolved,

If we were wise, against so great a foe
Contending, and so doubtful what might fall.
I laugh, when those who at the spear are bold
And venturous, if that fail them, shrink, and fear
What yet they know must follow — to endure
Exile, or ignominy, or bonds, or pain,
The sentence of their conqueror. This is now
Our doom; which if we can sustain and bear,
Our Supreme Foe in time may much remit 210
His anger, and perhaps, thus far removed,
Not mind us not offending, satisfied
With what is punished; whence these raging fires
Will slacken, if his breath stir not their flames.
Our purer essence then will overcome
Their noxious vapor, or, inured, not feel;
Or, changed at length, and to the place conformed
In temper and in nature, will receive
Familiar the fierce heat; and, void of pain,
This horror will grow mild, this darkness light; 220
Besides what hope the never-ending flight
Of future days may bring, what chance, what change
Worth waiting, — since our present lot appears
For happy though but ill, for ill not worst,
If we procure not to ourselves more woe.'
Thus Belial, with words clothed in reason's garb,
Counselled ignoble ease, and peaceful sloth,
Not peace; and after him thus Mammon spake: —
'Either to disenthrone the King of Heaven
We war, if war be best, or to regain 230
Our own right lost. Him to unthrone we then
May hope, when everlasting Fate shall yield
To fickle Chance, and Chaos judge the strife.
The former, vain to hope, argues as vain
The latter; for what place can be for us
Within Heaven's bound, unless Heaven's Lord Supreme

We overpower? Suppose he should relent,
And publish grace to all, on promise made
Of new subjection; with what eyes could we
Stand in his presence, humble, and receive 240
Strict laws imposed, to celebrate his throne
With warbled hymns, and to his Godhead sing
Forced Halleluiahs; while he lordly sits
Our envied sovran, and his altar breathes
Ambrosial odors and ambrosial flowers,
Our servile offerings? This must be our task
In Heaven, this our delight. How wearisome
Eternity so spent in worship paid
To whom we hate! Let us not then pursue,
By force impossible, by leave obtained 250
Unacceptable, though in Heaven, our state
Of splendid vassalage; but rather seek
Our own good from ourselves, and from our own
Live to ourselves, though in this vast recess,
Free, and to none accountable, preferring
Hard liberty before the easy yoke
Of servile pomp. Our greatness will appear
Then most conspicuous, when great things of small,
Useful of hurtful, prosperous of adverse,
We can create, and in what place soe'er 260
Thrive under evil, and work ease out of pain
Through labor and endurance. This deep world
Of darkness do we dread? How oft amidst
Thick clouds and dark doth Heaven's all-ruling Sire
Choose to reside, his glory unobscured,
And with the majesty of darkness round
Covers his throne, from whence deep thunders roar,
Mustering their rage, and Heaven resembles Hell!
As he our darkness, cannot we his light
Imitate when we please? This desert soil 270
Wants not her hidden lustre, gems and gold;

Nor want we skill or art, from whence to raise
Magnificence; and what can Heaven show more?
Our torments also may in length of time
Become our elements, these piercing fires
As soft as now severe, our temper changed
Into their temper; which must needs remove
The sensible of pain. All things invite
To peaceful counsels, and the settled state
Of order, how in safety best we may 280
Compose our present evils, with regard
Of what we are and where, dismissing quite
All thoughts of war. Ye have what I advise.'
He scarce had finished, when such murmur filled
The assembly, as when hollow rocks retain
The sound of blustering winds, which all night long
Had roused the sea, now with hoarse cadence lull
Seafaring men o'erwatched, whose bark by chance,
Or pinnace, anchors in a craggy bay
After the tempest: such applause was heard 290
As Mammon ended, and his sentence pleased,
Advising peace; for such another field
They dreaded worse than Hell; so much the fear
Of thunder and the sword of Michaël
Wrought still within them; and no less desire
To found this nether empire, which might rise,
By policy, and long process of time,
In emulation opposite to Heaven.
Which when Beëlzebub perceived, than whom,
Satan except, none higher sat, with grave 300
Aspect he rose, and in his rising seemed
A pillar of state; deep on his front engraven
Deliberation sat and public care;
And princely counsel in his face yet shone,
Majestic, though in ruin. Sage he stood,
With Atlantean shoulders fit to bear

The weight of mightiest monarchies; his look
Drew audience and attention still as night
Or summer's noontide air, while thus he spake: —
'Thrones and Imperial Powers, Offspring of Heaven, 310
Ethereal Virtues! or these titles now
Must we renounce, and, changing style, be called
Princes of Hell? for so the popular vote
Inclines — here to continue, and build up here
A growing empire; doubtless! while we dream,
And know not that the King of Heaven hath doomed
This place our dungeon, not our safe retreat
Beyond his potent arm, to live exempt
From Heaven's high jurisdiction, in new league
Banded against his throne, but to remain 320
In strictest bondage, though thus far removed,
Under the inevitable curb, reserved
His captive multitude. For he, be sure,
In highth or depth, still first and last will reign
Sole king, and of his kingdom lose no part
By our revolt, but over Hell extend
His empire, and with iron sceptre rule
Us here, as with his golden those in Heaven.
What sit we then projecting peace and war?
War hath determined us, and foiled with loss 330
Irreparable; terms of peace yet none
Vouchsafed or sought; for what peace will be given
To us enslaved, but custody severe,
And stripes, and arbitrary punishment
Inflicted? and what peace can we return,
But, to our power, hostility and hate,
Untamed reluctance, and revenge, though slow,
Yet ever plotting how the Conqueror least
May reap his conquest, and may least rejoice
In doing what we most in suffering feel? 340
Nor will occasion want, nor shall we need

With dangerous expedition to invade
Heaven, whose high walls fear no assault or siege,
Or ambush from the Deep. What if we find
Some easier enterprise? There is a place
(If ancient and prophetic fame in Heaven
Err not), another World, the happy seat
Of some new race called Man, about this time
To be created like to us, though less
In power and excellence, but favored more 350
Of him who rules above; so was his will
Pronounced among the gods, and by an oath
That shook Heaven's whole circumference, confirmed.
Thither let us bend all our thoughts, to learn
What creatures there inhabit, of what mould
Or substance, how endued, and what their power,
And where their weakness: how attempted best,
By force or subtlety. Though Heaven be shut,
And Heaven's high Arbitrator sit secure
In his own strength, this place may lie exposed, 360
The utmost border of his kingdom, left
To their defence who hold it; here, perhaps,
Some advantageous act may be achieved
By sudden onset: either with Hell-fire
To waste his whole creation, or possess
All as our own, and drive, as we are driven,
The puny habitants; or if not drive,
Seduce them to our party, that their God
May prove their foe, and with repenting hand
Abolish his own works. This would surpass 370
Common revenge, and interrupt his joy
In our confusion, and our joy upraise
In his disturbance; when his darling Sons,
Hurled headlong to partake with us, shall curse
Their frail original, and faded bliss —
Faded so soon! Advise if this be worth

Attempting, or to sit in darkness here
Hatching vain empires.' Thus Beëlzebub
Pleaded his devilish counsel, first devised
By Satan, and in part proposed; for whence, 380
But from the author of all ill, could spring
So deep a malice, to confound the race
Of Mankind in one root, and Earth with Hell
To mingle and involve, done all to spite
The great Creator? But their spite still serves
His glory to augment. The bold design
Pleased highly those infernal States, and joy
Sparkled in all their eyes; with full assent
They vote: whereat his speech he thus renews:—
'Well have ye judged, well ended long debate, 390
Synod of gods! and, like to what ye are,
Great things resolved; which from the lowest deep
Will once more lift us up, in spite of fate,
Nearer our ancient seat—perhaps in view
Of those bright confines, whence, with neighboring arms
And opportune excursion, we may chance
Re-enter Heaven; or else in some mild zone
Dwell not unvisited of Heaven's fair light,
Secure, and at the brightening orient beam
Purge off this gloom; the soft delicious air, 400
To heal the scar of these corrosive fires,
Shall breathe her balm. But first, whom shall we send
In search of this new World? whom shall we find
Sufficient? who shall tempt with wandering feet
The dark, unbottomed, infinite Abyss,
And through the palpable obscure find out
His uncouth way, or spread his aery flight,
Upborne with indefatigable wings
Over the vast abrupt, ere he arrive
The happy isle? What strength, what art, can then 410
Suffice, or what evasion bear him safe

Through the strict senteries and stations thick
Of Angels watching round? Here he had need
All circumspection: and we now no less
Choice in our suffrage; for on whom we send,
The weight of all, and our last hope, relies.
This said, he sat; and expectation held
His look suspense, awaiting who appeared
To second, or oppose, or undertake
The perilous attempt; but all sat mute, 420
Pondering the danger with deep thoughts; and each
In other's countenance read his own dismay,
Astonished. None among the choice and prime
Of those Heaven-warring champions could be found
So hardy as to proffer or accept,
Alone, the dreadful voyage; till at last
Satan, whom now transcendent glory raised
Above his fellows, with monarchal pride
Conscious of highest worth, unmoved thus spake:—
'O Progeny of Heaven! Empyreal Thrones! 430
With reason hath deep silence and demur
Seized us, though undismayed. Long is the way
And hard, that out of Hell leads up to Light;
Our prison strong, this huge convex of fire,
Outrageous to devour, immures us round
Ninefold; and gates of burning adamant,
Barred over us, prohibit all egress.
These passed, if any pass, the void profound
Of unessential Night receives him next,
Wide-gaping, and with utter loss of being 440
Threatens him, plunged in that abortive gulf.
If thence he scape into whatever world,
Or unknown region, what remains him less
Than unknown dangers and as hard escape?
But I should ill become this throne, O Peers,
And this imperial sovranty, adorned

With splendor, armed with power, if aught proposed
And judged of public moment, in the shape
Of difficulty or danger, could deter
Me from attempting. Wherefore do I assume 450
These royalties, and not refuse to reign,
Refusing to accept as great a share
Of hazard as of honor, due alike
To him who reigns, and so much to him due
Of hazard more, as he above the rest
High honored sits? Go therefore, mighty Powers,
Terror of Heaven, though fallen; intend at home,
While here shall be our home, what best may ease
The present misery, and render Hell
More tolerable; if there be cure or charm 460
To respite, or deceive, or slack the pain
Of this ill mansion; intermit no watch
Against a wakeful foe, while I abroad
Through all the coasts of dark destruction seek
Deliverance for us all: this enterprise
None shall partake with me.' Thus saying, rose
The Monarch, and prevented all reply;
Prudent, lest, from his resolution raised,
Others among the chief might offer now
(Certain to be refused) what erst they feared, 470
And, so refused, might in opinion stand
His rivals, winning cheap the high repute
Which he through hazard huge must earn. But they
Dreaded not more the adventure than his voice
Forbidding; and at once with him they rose;
The rising all at once was as the sound
Of thunder heard remote. Towards him they bend.
With awful reverence prone; and as a god
Extol him equal to the Highest in Heaven.
Nor failed they to express how much they praised 480
That for the general safety he despised

His own; for neither do the Spirits damned
Lose all their virtue; lest bad men should boast
Their specious deeds on Earth, which glory excites,
Or close ambition varnished o'er with zeal.
  Thus they their doubtful consultations dark
Ended, rejoicing in their matchless Chief;
As when from the mountain-tops the dusky clouds
Ascending, while the North-wind sleeps, o'erspread
Heaven's cheerful face, the louring element 490
Scowls o'er the darkened landskip snow or shower;
If chance the radiant sun with farewell sweet
Extend his evening beam, the fields revive,
The birds their notes renew, and bleating herds
Attest their joy, that hill and valley rings.
O shame to men! Devil with devil damned
Firm concord holds; men only disagree
Of creatures rational, though under hope
Of heavenly grace; and, God proclaiming peace,
Yet live in hatred, enmity, and strife 500
Among themselves, and levy cruel wars,
Wasting the Earth, each other to destroy:
As if (which might induce us to accord)
Man had not hellish foes enow besides,
That day and night for his destruction wait!
  The Stygian council thus dissolved; and forth
In order came the grand Infernal Peers;
Midst came their mighty Paramount, and seemed
Alone the antagonist of Heaven, nor less
Than Hell's dread Emperor, with pomp supreme, 510
And god-like imitated state; him round
A globe of fiery Seraphim enclosed
With bright emblazonry, and horrent arms.
Then of their session ended they bid cry
With trumpet's regal sound the great result:
Toward the four winds four speedy Cherubim

Put to their mouths the sounding alchymy,
By harald's voice explained; the hollow Abyss
Heard far and wide, and all the host of Hell
With deafening shout returned them loud acclaim. 520
Thence more at ease their minds, and somewhat raised
By false presumptuous hope, the ranged powers
Disband; and, wandering, each his several way
Pursues, as inclination or sad choice
Leads him perplexed, where he may likeliest find
Truce to his restless thoughts, and entertain
The irksome hours, till his great Chief return.
Part on the plain, or in the air sublime,
Upon the wing or in swift race contend,
As at the Olympian games or Pythian fields; 530
Part curb their fiery steeds, or shun the goal
With rapid wheels, or fronted brigads form:
As when, to warn proud cities, war appears
Waged in the troubled sky, and armies rush
To battle in the clouds; before each van
Prick forth the aery knights, and couch their spears,
Till thickest legions close; with feats of arms
From either end of Heaven the welkin burns.
Others, with vast Typhœan rage more fell,
Rend up both rocks and hills, and ride the air 540
In whirlwind; Hell scarce holds the wild uproar:
As when Alcides, from Œchalia crowned
With conquest, felt the envenomed robe, and tore
Through pain up by the roots Thessalian pines,
And Lichas from the top of Œta threw
Into the Euboic sea. Others, more mild,
Retreated in a silent valley, sing
With notes angelical to many a harp
Their own heroic deeds and hapless fall
By doom of battle; and complain that Fate 550
Free Virtue should enthrall to Force or Chance.

Their song was partial, but the harmony
(What could it less when Spirits immortal sing?)
Suspended Hell, and took with ravishment
The thronging audience. In discourse more sweet
(For eloquence the soul, song charms the sense)
Others apart sat on a hill retired,
In thoughts more elevate, and reasoned high
Of Providence, Foreknowledge, Will, and Fate,
Fixed fate, free will, foreknowledge absolute; 560
And found no end, in wandering mazes lost.
Of good and evil much they argued then,
Of happiness and final misery,
Passion and apathy, and glory and shame,
Vain wisdom all, and false philosophy! —
Yet with a pleasing sorcery could charm
Pain for a while or anguish, and excite
Fallacious hope, or arm the obdured breast
With stubborn patience as with triple steel.
Another part, in squadrons and gross bands, 570
On bold adventure to discover wide
That dismal world, if any clime perhaps
Might yield them easier habitation, bend
Four ways their flying march, along the banks
Of four infernal rivers that disgorge
Into the burning lake their baleful streams:
Abhorred Styx, the flood of deadly hate;
Sad Acheron of sorrow, black and deep;
Cocytus, named of lamentation loud
Heard on the rueful stream; fierce Phlegethon, 580
Whose waves of torrent fire inflame with rage.
Far off from these a slow and silent stream,
Lethe, the river of oblivion, rolls
Her watery labyrinth, whereof who drinks
Forthwith his former state and being forgets,
Forgets both joy and grief, pleasure and pain.

Beyond this flood a frozen continent
Lies dark and wild, beat with perpetual storms
Of whirlwind and dire hail, which on firm land
Thaws not, but gathers heap, and ruin seems 590
Of ancient pile; all else deep snow and ice,
A gulf profound as that Serbonian bog
Betwixt Damiata and Mount Casius old,
Where armies whole have sunk: the parching air
Burns frore, and cold performs the effect of fire.
Thither, by harpy-footed Furies haled,
At certain revolutions all the damned
Are brought; and feel by turns the bitter change
Of fierce extremes, extremes by change more fierce,
From beds of raging fire to starve in ice 600
Their soft ethereal warmth, and there to pine
Immovable, infixed, and frozen round
Periods of time; thence hurried back to fire.
They ferry over this Lethean sound
Both to and fro, their sorrow to augment,
And wish and struggle, as they pass, to reach
The tempting stream, with one small drop to lose
In sweet forgetfulness all pain and woe,
All in one moment, and so near the brink;
But Fate withstands, and, to oppose the attempt, 610
Medusa with Gorgonian terror guards
The ford, and of itself the water flies
All taste of living wight, as once it fled
The lip of Tantalus. Thus roving on
In confused march forlorn, the adventurous bands,
With shuddering horror pale, and eyes aghast,
Viewed first their lamentable lot, and found
No rest. Through many a dark and dreary vale
They passed, and many a region dolorous,
O'er many a frozen, many a fiery Alp, 620
Rocks, caves, lakes, fens, bogs, dens, and shades of death —

A universe of death, which God by curse
Created evil, for evil only good;
Where all life dies, death lives, and Nature breeds,
Perverse, all monstrous, all prodigious things,
Abominable, inutterable, and worse
Than fables yet have feigned, or fear conceived;
Gorgons, and Hydras, and Chimæras dire.
Meanwhile the Adversary of God and Man,
Satan, with thoughts inflamed of highest design, 630
Puts on swift wings, and toward the gates of Hell
Explores his solitary flight; sometimes
He scours the right hand coast, sometimes the left;
Now shaves with level wing the deep, then soars
Up to the fiery concave towering high.
As when far off at sea a fleet descried
Hangs in the clouds, by equinoctial winds
Close sailing from Bengala, or the isles
Of Ternate and Tidore, whence merchants bring
Their spicy drugs; they on the trading flood, 640
Through the wide Ethiopian to the Cape,
Ply stemming nightly toward the pole: so seemed
Far off the flying Fiend. At last appear
Hell-bounds, high reaching to the horrid roof,
And thrice threefold the gates; three folds were brass,
Three iron, three of adamantine rock,
Impenetrable, impaled with circling fire,
Yet unconsumed. Before the gates there sat
On either side a formidable Shape.
The one seemed woman to the waist, and fair, 650
But ended foul in many a scaly fold
Voluminous and vast, a serpent armed
With mortal sting. About her middle round
A cry of Hell-hounds never-ceasing barked
With wide Cerberean mouths full loud, and rung
A hideous peal; yet, when they list, would creep,

If aught disturbed their noise, into her womb,
And kennel there, yet there still barked and howled
Within unseen. Far less abhorred than these
Vexed Scylla, bathing in the sea that parts 660
Calabria from the hoarse Trinacrian shore;
Nor uglier follow the night-hag, when, called
In secret, riding through the air she comes,
Lured with the smell of infant blood, to dance
With Lapland witches, while the laboring moon
Eclipses at their charms. The other Shape —
If shape it might be called that shape had none
Distinguishable in member, joint, or limb;
Or substance might be called that shadow seemed,
For each seemed either — black it stood as Night, 670
Fierce as ten Furies, terrible as Hell,
And shook a dreadful dart; what seemed his head
The likeness of a kingly crown had on.
Satan was now at hand, and from his seat
The monster moving onward came as fast,
With horrid strides; Hell trembled as he strode.
The undaunted Fiend what this might be admired —
Admired, not feared; God and his Son except,
Created thing naught valued he nor shunned —
And with disdainful look thus first began: — 680
'Whence and what art thou, execrable Shape,
That darest, though grim and terrible, advance
Thy miscreated front athwart my way
To yonder gates? Through them I mean to pass,
That be assured, without leave asked of thee.
Retire; or taste thy folly, and learn by proof,
Hell-born, not to contend with Spirits of Heaven.'
To whom the Goblin, full of wrath, replied: —
'Art thou that Traitor-Angel, art thou he
Who first broke peace in Heaven and faith, till then 690
Unbroken, and in proud rebellious arms

Drew after him the third part of Heaven's sons,
Conjured against the Highest, for which both thou
And they, outcast from God, are here condemned
To waste eternal days in woe and pain?
And reckon'st thou thyself with Spirits of Heaven,
Hell-doomed, and breath'st defiance here and scorn,
Where I reign king, and, to enrage thee more,
Thy king and lord? Back to thy punishment,
False fugitive, and to thy speed add wings, 700
Lest with a whip of scorpions I pursue
Thy lingering, or with one stroke of this dart
Strange horror seize thee, and pangs unfelt before.'
So spake the grisly Terror, and in shape,
So speaking and so threatening, grew tenfold
More dreadful and deform. On the other side,
Incensed with indignation, Satan stood
Unterrified, and like a comet burned,
That fires the length of Ophiuchus huge
In the arctic sky, and from his horrid hair 710
Shakes pestilence and war. Each at the head
Levelled his deadly aim; their fatal hands
No second stroke intend; and such a frown
Each cast at the other, as when two black clouds,
With Heaven's artillery fraught, come rattling on
Over the Caspian, then stand front to front
Hovering a space, till winds the signal blow
To join their dark encounter in mid-air:—
So frowned the mighty combatants, that Hell
Grew darker at their frown; so matched they stood; 720
For never but once more was either like
To meet so great a foe. And now great deeds
Had been achieved, whereof all Hell had rung,
Had not the snaky Sorceress that sat
Fast by Hell-gate and kept the fatal key,
Risen, and with hideous outcry rushed between.

'O father, what intends thy hand,' she cried,
'Against thy only son? What fury, O son,
Possesses thee to bend that mortal dart
Against thy father's head? and know'st for whom? 730
For him who sits above, and laughs the while
At thee ordained his drudge, to execute
Whate'er his wrath, which he calls justice, bids—
His wrath, which one day will destroy ye both!'
She spake, and at her words the hellish Pest
Forbore: then these to her Satan returned:—
'So strange thy outcry, and thy words so strange
Thou interposest, that my sudden hand,
Prevented, spares to tell thee yet by deeds
What it intends, till first I know of thee 740
What thing thou art, thus double-formed, and why,
In this infernal vale first met, thou call'st
Me father, and that phantasm call'st my son.
I know thee not, nor ever saw till now
Sight more detestable than him and thee.'
To whom thus the Portress of Hell-gate replied:—
'Hast thou forgot me then, and do I seem
Now in thine eye so foul? once deemed so fair
In Heaven, when at the assembly, and in sight
Of all the Seraphim with thee combined 750
In bold conspiracy against Heaven's King,
All on a sudden miserable pain
Surprised thee; dim thine eyes, and dizzy swum
In darkness, while thy head flames thick and fast
Threw forth, till on the left side opening wide,
Likest to thee in shape and countenance bright,
Then shining heavenly fair, a goddess armed,
Out of thy head I sprung. Amazement seized
All the host of Heaven: back they recoiled afraid
At first, and called me *Sin*, and for a sign 760
Portentous held me; but, familiar grown,

I pleased, and with attractive graces won
The most averse; thee chiefly, who full oft
Thyself in me thy perfect image viewing
Becamest enamoured; and such joy thou took'st
With me in secret, that my womb conceived
A growing burden. Meanwhile war arose,
And fields were fought in Heaven; wherein remained
(For what could else?) to our Almighty Foe
Clear victory, to our part loss and rout 770
Through all the Empyrean. Down they fell,
Driven headlong from the pitch of Heaven, down
Into this deep; and in the general fall
I also: at which time this powerful key
Into my hands was given, with charge to keep
These gates forever shut, which none can pass
Without my opening. Pensive here I sat
Alone; but long I sat not, till my womb,
Pregnant by thee, and now excessive grown,
Prodigious motion felt and rueful throes. 780
At last this odious offspring whom thou seest,
Thine own begotten, breaking violent way,
Tore through my entrails, that, with fear and pain
Distorted, all my nether shape thus grew
Transformed; but he, my inbred enemy,
Forth issued, brandishing his fatal dart,
Made to destroy. I fled, and cried out *Death!*
Hell trembled at the hideous name, and sighed
From all her caves, and back resounded *Death!*
I fled; but he pursued (though more, it seems, 790
Inflamed with lust than rage) and, swifter far,
Me overtook, his mother, all dismayed,
And, in embraces forcible and foul
Engendering with me, of that rape begot
These yelling monsters, that with ceaseless cry
Surround me, as thou saw'st, hourly conceived

And hourly born, with sorrow infinite
To me; for, when they list, into the womb
That bred them they return, and howl, and gnaw
My bowels, their repast; then, bursting forth 800
Afresh, with conscious terrors vex me round,
That rest or intermission none I find.
Before mine eyes in opposition sits
Grim Death, my son and foe, who sets them on,
And me, his parent, would full soon devour
For want of other prey, but that he knows
His end with mine involved, and knows that I
Should prove a bitter morsel, and his bane,
Whenever that shall be: so Fate pronounced.
But thou, O father, I forewarn thee, shun 810
His deadly arrow; neither vainly hope
To be invulnerable in those bright arms,
Though tempered heavenly; for that mortal dint,
Save He who reigns above, none can resist.'

She finished; and the subtle Fiend his lore
Soon learned, now milder, and thus answered smooth: —

'Dear daughter — since thou claim'st me for thy sire,
And my fair son here show'st me, the dear pledge
Of dalliance had with thee in Heaven, and joys
Then sweet, now sad to mention, through dire change 820
Befallen us unforeseen, unthought of — know,
I come no enemy, but to set free
From out this dark and dismal house of pain
Both him and thee, and all the Heavenly host
Of Spirits that, in our just pretences armed,
Fell with us from on high. From them I go
This uncouth errand sole, and one for all
Myself expose, with lonely steps to tread
The unfounded Deep, and through the void immense
To search with wandering quest a place foretold 830
Should be — and by concurring signs, ere now

Created vast and round — a place of bliss
In the purlieus of Heaven; and therein placed
A race of upstart creatures, to supply
Perhaps our vacant room, though more removed,
Lest Heaven, surcharged with potent multitude,
Might hap to move new broils. Be this, or aught
Than this more secret, now designed, I haste
To know; and, this once known, shall soon return,
And bring ye to the place where thou and Death 840
Shall dwell at ease, and up and down unseen
Wing silently the buxom air, embalmed
With odors: there ye shall be fed and filled
Immeasurably; all things shall be your prey.'
He ceased; for both seemed highly pleased, and Death
Grinned horrible a ghastly smile, to hear
His famine should be filled, and blessed his maw
Destined to that good hour. No less rejoiced
His mother bad, and thus bespake her sire: —
'The key of this eternal pit, by due 850
And by command of Heaven's all-powerful King,
I keep, by Him forbidden to unlock
These adamantine gates; against all force
Death ready stands to interpose his dart,
Fearless to be o'ermatched by living might.
But what owe I to His commands above,
Who hates me, and hath hither thrust me down
Into this gloom of Tartarus profound,
To sit in hateful office here confined,
Inhabitant of Heaven and Heavenly-born, 860
Here in perpetual agony and pain,
With terrors and with clamors compassed round
Of mine own brood, that on my bowels feed?
Thou art my father, thou my author, thou
My being gavest me; whom should I obey
But thee? whom follow? Thou will bring me soon

To that new world of light and bliss, among
The gods who live at ease, where I shall reign
At thy right hand voluptuous, as beseems
Thy daughter and thy darling, without end.' 870
Thus saying, from her side the fatal key,
Sad instrument of all our woe, she took;
And, towards the gate rolling her bestial train,
Forthwith the huge portcullis high up-drew,
Which but herself not all the Stygian Powers
Could once have moved; then in the key-hole turns
The intricate wards, and every bolt and bar
Of massy iron or solid rock with ease
Unfastens: on a sudden open fly,
With impetuous recoil and jarring sound, 880
The infernal doors, and on their hinges grate
Harsh thunder, that the lowest bottom shook
Of Erebus. She opened; but to shut
Excelled her power: the gates wide open stood,
That with extended wings a bannered host,
Under spread ensigns marching, might pass through
With horse and chariots ranked in loose array;
So wide they stood, and like a furnace-mouth
Cast forth redounding smoke and ruddy flame.
Before their eyes in sudden view appear 890
The secrets of the hoary Deep, a dark
Illimitable ocean, without bound,
Without dimension; where length, breadth, and highth,
And time, and place, are lost; where eldest Night
And Chaos, ancestors of Nature, hold
Eternal anarchy, amidst the noise
Of endless wars, and by confusion stand.
For Hot, Cold, Moist, and Dry, four champions fierce,
Strive here for mastery, and to battle bring
Their embryon atoms; they around the flag 900
Of each his faction, in their several clans,

Light-armed or heavy, sharp, smooth, swift, or slow,
Swarm populous, unnumbered as the sands
Of Barca or Cyrene's torrid soil,
Levied to side with warring winds, and poise
Their lighter wings. To whom these most adhere,
He rules a moment; Chaos umpire sits,
And by decision more embroils the fray
By which he reigns; next him, high arbiter,
Chance governs all. Into this wild Abyss, 910
The womb of Nature, and perhaps her grave,
Of neither sea, nor shore, nor air, nor fire,
But all these in their pregnant causes mixed
Confusedly, and which thus must ever fight,
Unless the Almighty Maker them ordain
His dark materials to create more worlds —
Into this wild Abyss the wary Fiend
Stood on the brink of Hell and looked awhile,
Pondering his voyage; for no narrow frith
He had to cross. Nor was his ear less pealed 920
With noises loud and ruinous (to compare
Great things with small) than when Bellona storms
With all her battering engines, bent to rase
Some capital city; or less than if this frame
Of Heaven were falling, and these elements
In mutiny had from her axle torn
The steadfast Earth. At last his sail-broad vans
He spreads for flight, and in the surging smoke
Uplifted spurns the ground; thence many a league,
As in a cloudy chair, ascending rides 930
Audacious; but, that seat soon failing, meets
A vast vacuity: all unawares,
Fluttering his pennons vain, plumb-down he drops
Ten thousand fathom deep, and to this hour
Down had been falling, had not by ill chance
The strong rebuff of some tumultuous cloud,

Instinct with fire and nitre, hurried him
As many miles aloft: that fury stayed —
Quenched in a boggy Syrtis, neither sea,
Nor good dry land — nigh foundered, on he fares, 940
Treading the crude consistence, half on foot,
Half flying; behoves him now both oar and sail.
As when a gryphon through the wilderness
With winged course, o'er hill or moory dale,
Pursues the Arimaspian, who by stealth
Had from his wakeful custody purloined
The guarded gold: so eagerly the Fiend
O'er bog or steep, through strait, rough, dense, or rare,
With head, hands, wings, or feet, pursues his way,
And swims, or sinks, or wades, or creeps, or flies. 950
At length a universal hubbub wild
Of stunning sounds and voices all confused,
Borne through the hollow dark, assaults his ear
With loudest vehemence. Thither he plies
Undaunted, to meet there whatever Power
Or Spirit of the nethermost Abyss
Might in that noise reside, of whom to ask
Which way the nearest coast of darkness lies
Bordering on light; when straight behold the throne
Of *Chaos*, and his dark pavilion spread 960
Wide on the wasteful Deep! With him enthroned
Sat sable-vested *Night*, eldest of things,
The consort of his reign; and by them stood
Orcus and Ades, and the dreaded name
Of Demogorgon; Rumor next and Chance,
And Tumult and Confusion all embroiled,
And Discord with a thousand various mouths.
To whom Satan, turning boldly, thus: — 'Ye Powers
And Spirits of this nethermost Abyss,
Chaos and ancient Night, I come no spy, 970
With purpose to explore or to disturb

The secrets of your realm; but, by constraint
Wandering this darksome desert, as my way
Lies through your spacious empire up to light,
Alone and without guide, half lost, I seek
What readiest path leads where your gloomy bounds
Confine with Heaven; or if some other place,
From your dominion won, the Ethereal King
Possesses lately, thither to arrive
I travel this profound. Direct my course: 980
Directed, no mean recompense it brings
To your behoof, if I that region lost,
All usurpation thence expelled, reduce
To her original darkness and your sway
(Which is my present journey), and once more
Erect the standard there of ancient Night.
Yours be the advantage all, mine the revenge!'
Thus Satan; and him thus the Anarch old,
With faltering speech and visage incomposed,
Answered:—'I know thee, stranger, who thou art: 990
That mighty leading Angel, who of late
Made head against Heaven's King, though overthrown.
I saw and heard; for such a numerous host
Fled not in silence through the frighted deep,
With ruin upon ruin, rout on rout,
Confusion worse confounded; and Heaven-gates
Poured out by millions her victorious bands,
Pursuing. I upon my frontiers here
Keep residence; if all I can will serve
That little which is left so to defend, 1000
Encroached on still through our intestine broils
Weakening the sceptre of old Night: first Hell,
Your dungeon, stretching far and wide beneath;
Now lately Heaven and Earth, another world
Hung o'er my realm, linked in a golden chain
To that side Heaven from whence your legions fell.

If that way be your walk, you have not far;
So much the nearer danger. Go, and speed!
Havoc, and spoil, and ruin, are my gain.'
He ceased; and Satan stayed not to reply, 1010
But, glad that now his sea should find a shore,
With fresh alacrity and force renewed
Springs upward, like a pyramid of fire,
Into the wild expanse, and through the shock
Of fighting elements, on all sides round
Environed, wins his way; harder beset
And more endangered, than when Argo passed
Through Bosporus betwixt the justling rocks;
Or when Ulysses on the larboard shunned
Charybdis, and by the other whirlpool steered: 1020
So he with difficulty and labor hard
Moved on: with difficulty and labor he;
But, he once passed, soon after, when Man fell,
Strange alteration! Sin and Death amain,
Following his track (such was the will of Heaven)
Paved after him a broad and beaten way
Over the dark Abyss, whose boiling gulf
Tamely endured a bridge of wondrous length,
From Hell continued, reaching the utmost orb
Of this frail World; by which the Spirits perverse 1030
With easy intercourse pass to and fro
To tempt or punish mortals, except whom
God and good Angels guard by special grace.
But now at last the sacred influence
Of light appears, and from the walls of Heaven
Shoots far into the bosom of dim Night
A glimmering dawn. Here Nature first begins
Her farthest verge, and Chaos to retire,
As from her outmost works, a broken foe,
With tumult less and with less hostile din; 1040
That Satan with less toil, and now with ease,

Wafts on the calmer wave by dubious light,
And, like a weather-beaten vessel, holds
Gladly the port, though shrouds and tackle torn;
Or in the emptier waste, resembling air,
Weighs his spread wings, at leisure to behold
Far off the empyreal Heaven, extended wide
In circuit, undetermined square or round,
With opal towers, and battlements adorned
Of living sapphire, once his native seat; 1050
And, fast by, hanging in a golden chain,
This pendent World, in bigness as a star
Of smallest magnitude close by the moon.
Thither, full fraught with mischievous revenge,
Accurst, and in a cursed hour, he hies.

CONCLUSION.

The first two books constitute an interlude, or perhaps rather a link, between the two tragic motives of the poem: the fall of Satan, and the fall of Adam. Interest is to be sustained in the preceding action upon the vast stage of infinity by the very act of advance towards that limited field of Adam's struggle. The greater portion of the opening books is devoted to the delineation of the character of Satan and of his principal associates; it is only toward the close of the second book that, in the departure of Satan from Pandemonium, the former action is resumed and the latter assumed. Henceforth the arena of action is to be steadily narrowed, to the stellar universe, to the earth, to the country of Eden, and finally to that fateful garden in which human and heavenly and infernal powers are to meet and make their first sad adjustment.

> Now had the Almighty Father from above,
> From the pure Empyrean where he sits
> High throned above all highth, bent down his eye,
> His own works and their works at once to view:
> Above him all the Sanctities of Heaven
> Stood thick as stars, and from his sight received
> Beatitude past utterance; on his right
> The radiant image of his glory sat,
> His only Son. On Earth he first beheld
> Our two first parents, yet the only two
> Of mankind, in the happy garden placed,

Reaping immortal fruits of joy and love,
Uninterrupted joy, unrivalled love,
In blissful solitude. He then surveyed
Hell and the gulf between, and Satan there
Coasting the wall of Heaven on this side Night,
In the dun air sublime, and ready now
To stoop with wearied wings and willing feet
On the bare outside of this World, that seemed
Firm land embosomed, without firmament,
Uncertain which, in ocean or in air.

(III. 56–76.)

In point of space, the action is to be gradually contracted; but presently we are given a further vista of its scope in point of time. The Father, communing with the Son,

foretells the success of Satan in perverting mankind; clears his own justice and wisdom from all imputation, having created Man free and able enough to have withstood his tempter; yet declares his purpose of grace towards him, in regard he fell not of his own malice, as did Satan, but by him seduced. The Son of God renders praises to his Father for the manifestation of his gracious purpose towards Man; but God again declares that grace cannot be extended towards Man without the satisfaction of divine justice; Man hath offended the Majesty of God by aspiring to Godhead, and, therefore, with all his progeny, devoted to death, must die, unless some one can be found sufficient to answer for his offence, and undergo his punishment. The Son of God freely offers himself a ransom for Man; the Father accepts him, ordains his incarnation, pronounces his exaltation above all names in Heaven and Earth; commands all the Angels to adore him; they obey, and hymning to their harps in full choir, celebrate the Father and the Son.

(Argument, Bk. III.)

Thus they in Heaven, above the Starry Sphere,
Their happy hours in joy and hymning spent.
Meanwhile upon the firm opacous globe
Of this round World, whose first convex divides

The luminous inferior orbs, enclosed
From Chaos and the inroad of Darkness old,
Satan alighted walks. A globe far off
It seemed, now seems a boundless continent,
Dark, waste, and wild, under the frown of Night
Starless exposed, and ever-threatening storms
Of Chaos blustering round, inclement sky,
Save on that side which from the wall of Heaven,
Though distant far, some small reflection gains
Of glimmering air less vexed with tempest loud:
Here walked the Fiend at large in spacious field.
As when a vulture on Imaus bred,
Whose snowy ridge the roving Tartar bounds,
Dislodging from a region scarce of prey,
To gorge the flesh of lambs or yeanling kids
On hills where flocks are fed, flies toward the springs
Of Ganges or Hydaspes, Indian streams;
But in his way lights on the barren plains
Of Sericana, where Chineses drive
With sails and wind their cany wagons light:
So on this windy sea of land, the Fiend
Walked up and down alone, bent on his prey:
Alone; for other creature in this place,
Living or lifeless, to be found was none.

(III. 416–443.)

Passing over this vast unpeopled tract, Satan's eye is at last caught by a distant gleam, which, upon nearer approach, he perceives to be the shining gate of Heaven, down from which extends a passage to an opening in the shell of the stellar World, or universe, and farther, to earth itself.

Satan from hence, now on the lower stair
That scaled by steps of gold to Heaven gate,
Looks down with wonder at the sudden view
Of all this World at once. As when a scout
Through dark and desert ways with peril gone
All night, at last by break of cheerful dawn

Obtains the brow of some high-climbing hill,
Which to his eye discovers unaware
The goodly prospect of some foreign land
First seen, or some renowned metropolis
With glistering spires and pinnacles adorned,
Which now the rising Sun gilds with his beams:
Such wonder seized, though after Heaven seen,
The Spirit malign, but much more envy seized,
At sight of all this World beheld so fair.
Round he surveys (and well might, where he stood
So high above the circling canopy
Of Night's extended shade) from eastern point
Of Libra to the fleecy star that bears
Andromeda far off Atlantic seas
Beyond the horizon; then from pole to pole
He views in breadth, and without longer pause
Down right into the World's first region throws
His flight precipitant, and winds with ease
Through the pure marble air his oblique way
Amongst innumerable stars, that shone
Stars distant, but nigh-hand seemed other worlds;
Or other worlds they seemed, or happy isles,
Like those Hesperian gardens famed of old,
Fortunate fields, and groves, and flowery vales,
Thrice happy isles! But who dwelt happy there
He stayed not to inquire: above them all
The golden Sun, in splendor likest Heaven,
Allured his eye: thither his course he bends
Through the calm firmament (but up or down,
By centre, or eccentric, hard to tell,
Or longitude) where the great luminary
Aloof the vulgar constellations thick,
That from his lordly eye keep distance due,
Dispenses light from far.

(III. 540–579.)

Here Satan alights, and, scanning the clear landscape, in which is no shadow, he presently descries another being, whom he recognizes as one of the sons of God.

His back was turned, but not his brightness hid:
Of beaming sunny rays a golden tiar
Circled his head, nor less his locks behind
Illustrious on his shoulders fledge with wings
Lay waving round. On some great charge employed
He seemed, or fixed in cogitation deep.
Glad was the Spirit impure, as now in hope
To find who might direct his wandering flight
To Paradise, the happy seat of Man,
His journey's end, and our beginning woe.
But first he casts to change his proper shape,
Which else might work him danger or delay:
And now a stripling Cherub he appears,
Not of the prime, yet such as in his face
Youth smiled celestial, and to every limb
Suitable grace diffused, so well he feigned:
Under a coronet his flowing hair
In curls on either cheek played; wings he wore
Of many a colored plume, sprinkled with gold;
His habit fit for speed succinct, and held
Before his decent steps a silver wand.
He drew not nigh unheard: the Angel bright,
Ere he drew nigh, his radiant visage turned,
Admonished by his ear, and straight was known
The Archangel Uriel, one of the seven
Who in God's presence, nearest to his throne,
Stand ready at command.

(III. 624–650.)

Safe in his disguise, Satan boldly accosts his former foe, asserts that he has wandered from Heaven in the hope of beholding the wonderful new creature of the divine power; and asks Uriel to direct him to the home of Man. Uriel praises the supposed angel for his zeal, and pictures to him the grandeur of God's might, and its evidencing in the act of creation just accomplished, of which he has been eye-witness:

'I saw when at his word the formless mass,
This World's material mould, came to a heap:

Confusion heard his voice, and wild Uproar
Stood ruled, stood vast Infinitude confined;
Till, at his second bidding, Darkness fled,
Light shone, and Order from Disorder sprung:
Swift to their several quarters hasted then
The cumbrous elements, Earth, Flood, Air, Fire;
And this ethereal quintessence of Heaven
Flew upward, spirited with various forms,
That rolled orbicular, and turned to stars
Numberless, as thou seest, and how they move:
Each had his place appointed, each his course;
The rest in circuit walls this Universe.
Look downward on that globe, whose hither side
With light from hence, though but reflected, shines;
That place is Earth, the seat of Man; that light
His day, which else, as the other hemisphere,
Night would invade; but there the neighboring moon
(So call that opposite fair star) her aid
Timely interposes, and her monthly round
Still ending, still renewing, through mid-heaven,
With borrowed light her countenance triform
Hence fills and empties to enlighten the Earth,
And in her pale dominion checks the night.
That spot to which I point is Paradise,
Adam's abode, those lofty shades his bower.
Thy way thou canst not miss, me mine requires.'
  Thus said, he turned; and Satan bowing low,
As to superior Spirits is wont in Heaven,
Where honor due and reverence none neglects,
Took leave, and toward the coast of earth beneath,
Down from the ecliptic, sped with hoped success,
Throws his steep flight in many an aery wheel,
Nor stayed, till on Niphates' top he lights.

(III. 708–742.)

Success is now at hand; Satan already feels that the prey is at his mercy. But he has one or two battles yet to fight with his better nature, before the not ignoble pride which inspires his thirst for vengeance becomes degraded into mere malice and foul, because consciously nourished, hatred of everything good and pure and true. He approaches earth and Eden and the pair who are to suffer through him, with confidence:

> Yet not rejoicing in his speed, though bold
> Far off, and fearless; nor with cause to boast
> Begins his dire attempt; which nigh the birth
> Now rolling, boils in his tumultuous breast,
> And like a devilish engine back recoils
> Upon himself: horror and doubt distract
> His troubled thoughts, and from the bottom stir
> The Hell within him; for within him Hell
> He brings, and round about him; nor from Hell
> One step no more than from himself can fly
> By change of place: now Conscience wakes Despair
> That slumbered; wakes the bitter memory
> Of what he was, what is, and what must be
> Worse; of worse deeds worse sufferings must ensue.
> Sometimes towards Eden, which now in his view
> Lay pleasant, his grieved look he fixes sad;
> Sometimes towards Heaven and the full-blazing Sun,
> Which now sat high in his meridian tower:
> Then, much revolving, thus in sighs began:—
> 'O thou that, with surpassing glory crowned,
> Look'st from thy sole dominion like the god
> Of this new World — at whose sight all the stars
> Hide their diminished heads — to thee I call,
> But with no friendly voice, and add thy name,
> O Sun, to tell thee how I hate thy beams,
> That bring to my remembrance from what state
> I fell, how glorious once above thy sphere;
> Till pride and worse ambition threw me down,
> Warring in Heaven against Heaven's matchless King:
> Ah wherefore? He deserved no such return
> From me, whom he created what I was
> In that bright eminence, and with his good

Upbraided none; nor was his service hard.
What could be less than to afford him praise,
The easiest recompense, and pay him thanks,
How due! Yet all his good proved ill in me,
And wrought but malice; lifted up so high,
I sdained subjection, and thought one step higher
Would set me highest, and in a moment quit
The debt immense of endless gratitude,
So burdensome still paying, still to owe,
Forgetful what from Him I still received,
And understood not that a grateful mind
By owing owes not, but still pays, at once
Indebted and discharged: what burden then?
O had his powerful destiny ordained
Me some inferior Angel, I had stood
Then happy; no unbounded hope had raised
Ambition. Yet, why not? Some other Power,
As great might have aspired, and me, though mean,
Drawn to his part; but other Powers as great
Fell not, but stand unshaken, from within
Or from without, to all temptations armed.
Hadst thou the same free will and power to stand?
Thou hadst. Whom hast thou then or what to accuse
But Heaven's free love dealt equally to all?
Be then his love accursed, since, love or hate,
To me alike it deals eternal woe.
Nay, cursed be thou; since against his thy will
Chose freely what it now so justly rues.
Me miserable! which way shall I fly
Infinite wrath, and infinite despair?
Which way I fly is Hell; myself am Hell;
And in the lowest deep a lower deep
Still threatening to devour me opens wide,
To which the Hell I suffer seems a Heaven.
O then at last relent! Is there no place
Left for repentance, none for pardon left?
None left but by submission; and that word
Disdain forbids me, and my dread of shame
Among the Spirits beneath, whom I seduced

With other promises and other vaunts
Than to submit, boasting I could subdue
The Omnipotent. Ay me, they little know
How dearly I abide that boast so vain,
Under what torments inwardly I groan.
While they adore me on the throne of Hell,
With diadem and sceptre high advanced,
The lower still I fall, only supreme
In misery: such joy ambition finds!
But say I could repent, and could obtain,
By act of grace, my former state; how soon
Would highth recall high thoughts, how soon unsay
What feigned submission swore! Ease would recant
Vows made in pain, as violent and void
(For never can true reconcilement grow
Where wounds of deadly hate have pierced so deep);
Which would but lead me to a worse relapse
And heavier fall: so should I purchase dear
Short intermission, bought with double smart.
This knows my Punisher; therefore as far
From granting he, as I from begging, peace.
All hope excluded thus, behold, instead
Of us, outcast, exiled, his new delight,
Mankind, created, and for him this World!
So farewell hope, and with hope farewell fear,
Farewell remorse! All good to me is lost;
Evil, be thou my good: by thee, at least
Divided empire with Heaven's King I hold,
By thee, and more than half perhaps will reign;
As Man erelong, and this new World, shall know.'
  Thus while he spake, each passion dimmed his face;
Thrice changed with pale, ire, envy, and despair;
Which marred his borrowed visage, and betrayed
Him counterfeit, if any eye beheld.
For heavenly minds from such distempers foul
Are ever clear. Whereof he soon aware,
Each perturbation smoothed with outward calm,
Artificer of fraud; and was the first
That practised falsehood under saintly show,

Deep malice to conceal, couched with revenge:
Yet not enough had practised to deceive
Uriel once warned; whose eye pursued him down
The way he went, and on the Assyrian mount
Saw him disfigured more than could befall
Spirit of happy sort; his gestures fierce
He marked and mad demeanor, then alone,
As he supposed, all unobserved, unseen.
So on he fares, and to the border comes
Of Eden, where delicious Paradise,
Now nearer, crowns with her enclosure green,
As with a rural mound, the champain head
Of a steep wilderness, whose hairy sides
With thicket overgrown, grotesque and wild,
Access denied; and overhead up grew
Insuperable highth of loftiest shade,
Cedar, and pine, and fir, and branching palm;
A sylvan scene; and as the ranks ascend,
Shade above shade, a woody theatre
Of stateliest view.

(IV. 16-142.)

Satan approaches, and, disdaining to seek an entrance by the gate, bounds over the verdurous wall, and flies at once to the most elevated place in the garden, the topmost branch of the Tree of Life.

Beneath him, with new wonder, now he views
To all delight of human sense exposed
In narrow room Nature's whole wealth; yea, more,
A Heaven on Earth: for blissful Paradise
Of God the garden was, by him in the east
Of Eden planted; Eden stretched her line
From Auran eastward to the royal towers
Of great Seleucia, built by Grecian kings,
Or where the sons of Eden long before
Dwelt in Telassar. In this pleasant soil
His far more pleasant garden God ordained;

> Out of the fertile ground he caused to grow
> All trees of noblest kind for sight, smell, taste;
> And all amid them stood the Tree of Life,
> High eminent, blooming ambrosial fruit
> Of vegetable gold; and next to life,
> Our death, the Tree of Knowledge, grew fast by —
> Knowledge of good, bought dear by knowing ill.
> (IV. 205-222.)

Nearer at hand are brooks, which,

> Rolling on orient pearl and sands of gold,
> With mazy error under pendent shades
> Ran nectar, visiting each plant.

But none of these scenes of beauty move Satan to pleasure:

> The Fiend
> Saw undelighted all delight, all kind
> Of living creatures, new to sight and strange.
> Two of far nobler shape, erect and tall,
> Godlike erect, with native honor clad
> In naked majesty seemed lords of all,
> And worthy seemed; for in their looks divine
> The image of their glorious Maker shone,
> Truth, wisdom, sanctitude severe and pure
> (Severe, but in true filial freedom placed),
> Whence true authority in men: though both
> Not equal, as their sex not equal seemed:
> For contemplation he and valor formed;
> For softness she, and sweet attractive grace;
> He for God only, she for God in him.
> His fair large front and eye sublime declared
> Absolute rule; and hyacinthine locks
> Round from his parted forelock manly hung
> Clustering, but not beneath his shoulders broad:
> She, as a veil down to the slender waist,
> Her unadorned golden tresses wore
> Dishevelled, but in wanton ringlets waved,

As the vine curls her tendrils; which implied
Subjection, but required with gentle sway,
And by her yielded, by him best received
Yielded, with coy submission, modest pride,
And sweet, reluctant, amorous delay.

(IV. 285-311.)

At sight of the pair Satan once more experiences a momentary revulsion from his purpose, but with no real hesitation as to his course; and an easy bit of sophistry very quickly restores him to himself. He is not their foe, after all, he says, apostrophizing them:

'League with you I seek,
And mutual amity so strait, so close,
That I with you must dwell, or you with me,
Henceforth. My dwelling haply may not please,
Like this fair Paradise, your sense; yet such
Accept your Maker's work; he gave it me,
Which I as freely give: Hell shall unfold,
To entertain you two, her widest gates,
And send forth all her kings; there will be room,
Not like these narrow limits, to receive
Your numerous offspring; if no better place,
Thank him who puts me, loath, to this revenge
On you who wrong me not, for him who wronged.
And should I at your harmless innocence
Melt, as I do, yet public reason just—
Honor and empire with revenge enlarged
By conquering this new World — compels me now
To do what else, though damned, I should abhor.'
So spake the Fiend, and with necessity,
The tyrant's plea, excused his devilish deeds.

(IV. 375-394.)

In the meantime Uriel reports to his superior, Gabriel, the circumstance of the meeting with the stranger, his departure toward earth, and his suspicious behavior upon the mountain-top. Gabriel commends Uriel for his vigilance, and agrees with him that measures must be taken to discover and oust the stranger, if he should prove, as they suspect, to be one of the fallen spirits.

> Now came still Evening on, and Twilight gray
> Had in her sober livery all things clad;
> Silence accompanied: for beast and bird,
> They to their grassy couch, these to their nests,
> Were slunk, all but the wakeful nightingale:
> She all night long her amorous descant sung:
> Silence was pleased. Now glowed the firmament
> With living sapphires: Hesperus, that led
> The starry host, rode brightest, till the moon,
> Rising in clouded majesty, at length
> Apparent queen, unveiled her peerless light,
> And o'er the dark her silver mantle threw.
>
> (IV. 598-609.)

Gabriel, to whom has been given main charge of guarding the new creation, and especially Adam and Eve, sends out certain of his subordinates to search in the garden for the suspected stranger. They find Satan squatting in the form of a toad at the ear of the sleeping Eve. Surprised, and for the moment overawed by the splendor and God-given authority of the Angels, he suffers himself to be led before Gabriel:

> To whom with stern regard thus Gabriel spake:
> 'Why hast thou, Satan, broke the bounds prescribed
> To thy transgressions, and disturbed the charge
> Of others, who approve not to transgress
> By thy example, but have power and right
> To question thy bold entrance on this place;
> Employed it seems to violate sleep, and those
> Whose dwelling God hath planted here in bliss?'
> To whom thus Satan with contemptuous brow:—
> 'Gabriel, thou hadst in Heaven the esteem of wise,
> And such I held thee; but this question asked

Puts me in doubt. Lives there who loves his pain?
Who would not, finding way, break loose from Hell,
Though thither doomed? Thou would'st thyself, no doubt,
And boldly venture to whatever place
Farthest from pain, where thou might'st hope to change
Torment with ease, and soonest recompense
Dole with delight, which in this place I sought;
To thee no reason, who knowest only good,
But evil hast not tried. And wilt object
His will who bound us? Let him surer bar
His iron gates, if he intends our stay
In that dark durance: thus much what was asked.
The rest is true; they found me where they say;
But that implies not violence or harm.'
  Thus he in scorn. The warlike Angel, moved,
Disdainfully, half smiling, thus replied:—
'O loss of one in Heaven to judge of wise,
Since Satan fell, whom folly overthrew,
And now returns him from his prison scaped,
Gravely in doubt whether to hold them wise
Or not, who ask what boldness brought him hither,
Unlicensed from his bounds in Hell prescribed!
So wise he judges it to fly from pain,
However, and to scape his punishment.
So judge thou still, presumptuous, till the wrath,
Which thou incurrest by flying, meet thy flight
Sevenfold, and scourge that wisdom back to Hell
Which taught thee yet no better, that no pain
Can equal anger infinite provoked.
But wherefore thou alone? Wherefore with thee
Came not all Hell broke loose? Is pain to them
Less pain, less to be fled? or thou than they
Less hardy to endure? Courageous Chief,
The first in flight from pain, hadst thou alleged
To thy deserted host this cause of flight,
Thou surely hadst not come sole fugitive.'
  To which the Fiend thus answered, frowning stern:—
'Not that I less endure, or shrink from pain,
Insulting Angel: well thou knowest I stood

Thy fiercest, when in battle to thy aid
The blasting volleyed thunder made all speed,
And seconded thy else not dreaded spear.
But still thy words at random, as before,
Argue thy inexperience what behoves
From hard essays and ill successes past,
A faithful leader — not to hazard all
Through ways of danger by himself untried:
I therefore, I alone, first undertook
To wing the desolate Abyss, and spy
This new-created World, whereof in Hell
Fame is not silent, here in hope to find
Better abode, and my afflicted Powers
To settle here on earth, or in mid-air;
Though for possession put to try once more
What thou and thy gay legions dare against;
Whose easier business were to serve their Lord
High up in Heaven, with songs to hymn his throne,
And practised distances to cringe, not fight.'
To whom the warrior Angel soon replied: —
'To say and straight unsay, pretending first
Wise to fly pain, professing next the spy,
Argues no leader, but a liar traced,
Satan; and couldst thou "faithful" add? O name,
O sacred name of faithfulness profaned!
Faithful to whom? to thy rebellious crew?
Army of Fiends, fit body to fit head!
Was this your discipline and faith engaged,
Your military obedience, to dissolve
Allegiance to the acknowledged Power Supreme?
And thou, sly hypocrite, who now wouldst seem
Patron of liberty, who more than thou
Once fawned, and cringed, and servilely adored
Heaven's awful Monarch? wherefore but in hope
To dispossess him, and thyself to reign?
But mark what I areed thee now: Avaunt!
Fly thither whence thou fledd'st: if from this hour
Within these hallowed limits thou appear,
Back to the infernal pit I drag thee chained,

And seal thee so as henceforth not to scorn
The facile gates of Hell too slightly barred.'
So threatened he; but Satan to no threats
Gave heed, but, waxing more in rage, replied: —
'Then when I am thy captive, talk of chains,
Proud limitary Cherub; but ere then
Far heavier load thyself expect to feel
From my prevailing arm, though Heaven's King
Ride on thy wings, and thou with thy compeers,
Used to the yoke, draw'st his triumphant wheels
In progress through the road of Heaven star-paved.'
While thus he spake, the angelic squadron bright
Turned fiery red, sharpening in mooned horns
Their phalanx, and began to hem him round
With ported spears, as thick as when a field
Of Ceres ripe for harvest waving bends
Her bearded grove of ears, which way the wind
Sways them; the careful ploughman doubting stands,
Lest on the threshing-floor his hopeful sheaves
Prove chaff. On the other side Satan, alarmed,
Collecting all his might, dilated stood,
Like Teneriff or Atlas, unremoved:
His stature reached the sky, and on his crest
Sat Horror plumed; nor wanted in his grasp
What seemed both spear and shield. Now dreadful deeds
Might have ensued; nor only Paradise
In this commotion, but the starry cope
Of Heaven perhaps, or all the elements
At least had gone to wrack, disturbed and torn
With violence of this conflict, had not soon
The Eternal, to prevent such horrid fray,
Hung forth in Heaven his golden scales, yet seen
Betwixt Astræa and the Scorpion sign,
Wherein all things created first he weighed,
The pendulous round earth with balanced air
In counterpoise; now ponders all events,
Battles, and realms: in these he put two weights,
The sequel each of parting and of fight;
The latter quick up flew, and kicked the beam;

> Which Gabriel spying, thus bespake the Fiend:—
> 'Satan, I know thy strength, and thou know'st mine;
> Neither our own, but given. What folly then
> To boast what arms can do? since thine no more
> Than Heaven permits, nor mine, though doubled now
> To trample thee as mire: for proof, look up,
> And read thy lot in yon celestial sign,
> Where thou art weighed, and shown how light, how weak,
> If thou resist.' The Fiend looked up, and knew
> His mounted scale aloft: nor more; but fled
> Murmuring; and with him fled the shades of night.
>
> (IV. 876–1015.)

With the morning Eve wakes to tell Adam of a strange dream, in which she has been led to the Tree of Knowledge, and there persuaded by a heavenly visitant (as she supposes), to taste its forbidden fruit. Adam comforts and reassures her, and, lifting a hymn of praise, they go about their daily tasks. That there may be no doubt that man is responsible for his fall, God sends the archangel Raphael to warn them explicitly against the wiles of Satan. The Seraph is welcomed by Adam and Eve with wonder and delight; delivers his warning; and, in reply to their questions, rehearses the story of the great strife in Heaven, the defeat and expulsion of the rebel Angels, Satan's persistence in his crime against God, and his consequent enmity to man.

In the meantime, Satan, cast out of Eden, wanders restlessly about, compassing the globe; and at length re-enters the garden, in the form of a mist. Casting about for a new disguise fit for the pursuance of his designs against humanity, he has determined to enter into the form of the serpent; not without qualms of shame and desperation:—

> 'O foul descent! that I, who erst contended
> With Gods to sit the highest, am now constrained
> Into a beast, and, mixed with bestial slime,

This essence to incarnate and imbrute,
That to the highth of deity aspired!
But what will not ambition and revenge
Descend to? Who aspires, must down as low
As high he soared, obnoxious first or last
To basest things. Revenge, at first though sweet,
Bitter erelong back on itself recoils.
Let it: I reck not, so it light well aimed,
Since higher I fall short, on him who next
Provokes my envy, this new favorite
Of Heaven, this man of clay, son of despite,
Whom us the more to spite his Maker raised
From dust. Spite then with spite is best repaid.'
So saying, through each thicket dank or dry,
Like a black mist low creeping, he held on
His midnight search, where soonest he might find
The serpent: him fast sleeping soon he found,
In labyrinth of many a round self-rolled,
His head the midst, well stored with subtle wiles
Nor yet in horrid shade or dismal den,
Nor nocent yet, but on the grassy herb
Fearless, unfeared, he slept. In at his mouth
The devil entered; and his brutal sense,
In heart or head, possessing, soon inspired
With act intelligential; but his sleep
Disturbed not, waiting close the approach of morn.

(IX. 163–191.)

Dawn comes, and Adam and Eve once more give praise to the Creator, and take up the simple round of their daily life. Eve suggests that their duties make it advisable for them to work separately. Adam holds that they are safer together, and reminds her of the warning to strict vigilance which the Seraph has but now given them. Eve, piqued that she should be considered lacking in strength to withstand temptation, urges more warmly her preference; and Adam after some debate, and a vain effort to dissuade her, suffers her to leave him.

Her long with ardent look his eye pursued,
Delighted; but desiring more her stay.
Oft he to her his charge of quick return
Repeated; she to him as oft engaged
To be returned by noon amid the bower,
And all things in best order to invite
Noontide repast, or afternoon's repose.
O much deceived, much failing, hapless Eve,
Of thy presumed return! event perverse!
Thou never from that hour in Paradise
Found'st either sweet repast or sound repose!
Such ambush hid among sweet flowers and shades
Waited with hellish rancor imminent
To intercept thy way, or send thee back
Despoiled of innocence, of faith, of bliss.
For now, and since first break of dawn, the Fiend,
Mere serpent in appearance, forth was come,
And on his quest, where likeliest he might find
The only two of mankind, but in them
The whole included race; his purposed prey.
In bower and field he sought, where any tuft
Of grove or garden-plot more pleasant lay,
Their tendance or plantation for delight:
By fountain, or by shady rivulet
He sought them both; but wished his hap might find
Eve separate; he wished, but not with hope
Of what so seldom chanced, when to his wish,
Beyond his hope, Eve separate he spies,
Veiled in a cloud of fragrance, where she stood,
Half spied, so thick the roses blushing round
About her glowed, oft stooping to support
Each flower of slender stalk, whose head, though gay
Carnation, purple, azure, or specked with gold,
Hung drooping unsustained: them she upstays
Gently with myrtle band, mindless the while
Herself, though fairest unsupported flower,
From her best prop so far, and storm so nigh.
Nearer he drew; and many a walk traversed
Of stateliest covert, cedar, pine, or palm,

Then voluble and bold, now hid, now seen
Among thick-woven arborets and flowers
Imbordered on each bank, the hand of Eve:
Spot more delicious than those gardens feigned
Or of revived Adonis, or renowned
Alcinous, host of old Laertes' son,
Or that, not mystic, where the sapient king
Held dalliance with his fair Egyptian spouse.
Much he the place admired, the person more,
As one who, long in populous city pent,
Where houses thick, and sewers, annoy the air,
Forth issuing on a summer's morn, to breathe
Among the pleasant villages and farms
Adjoined, from each thing met conceives delight —
The smell of grain, or tedded grass, or kine,
Or dairy, each rural sight, each rural sound —
If chance with nymph-like step fair virgin pass,
What pleasing seemed, for her now pleases more,
She most, and in her look sums all delight:
Such pleasure took the serpent to behold
This flowery plat, the sweet recess of Eve,
Thus early, thus alone. Her heavenly form,
Angelic, but more soft and feminine,
Her graceful innocence, her every air
Of gesture or least action, overawed
His malice, and with rapine sweet bereaved
His fierceness of the fierce intent it brought.
That space the Evil One abstracted stood
From his own evil, and for the time remained
Stupidly good; of enmity disarmed,
Of guile, of hate, of envy, of revenge.
But the hot Hell that always in him burns,
Though in mid Heaven, soon ended his delight,
And tortures him now more, the more he sees
Of pleasure not for him ordained. Then soon
Fierce hate he recollects, and all his thoughts
Of mischief, gratulating, thus excites: —
'Thoughts, whither have ye led me? With what sweet
Compulsion thus transported to forget

What hither brought us? hate, not love, nor hope
Of Paradise for Hell, hope here to taste
Of pleasure; but all pleasure to destroy,
Save what is in destroying; other joy
To me is lost. Then let me not let pass
Occasion, which now smiles. Behold alone
The woman, opportune to all attempts—
Her husband, for I view far round, not nigh,
Whose higher intellectual more I shun,
And strength, of courage haughty, and of limb
Heroic built, though of terrestrial mould;
Foe not informidable, exempt from wound—
I not; so much hath Hell debased, and pain
Enfeebled me, to what I was in Heaven.
She fair, divinely fair, fit love for Gods,
Not terrible, though terror be in love
And beauty, not approached by stronger hate,
Hate stronger, under show of love well feigned;
The way which to her ruin now I tend.'

So spake the enemy of mankind, enclosed
In serpent, inmate bad, and toward Eve
Addressed his way, not with indented wave,
Prone on the ground, as since, but on his rear
Circular base of rising folds, that towered
Fold above fold a surging maze, his head
Crested aloft, and carbuncle his eyes;
With burnished neck of verdant gold, erect
Amidst his circling spires, that on the grass
Floated redundant. Pleasing was his shape,
And lovely: never since the serpent kind
Lovelier: not those that in Illyria changed
Hermione and Cadmus, or the God
In Epidaurus; nor to which transformed
Ammonian Jove, or Capitoline was seen;
He with Olympias, this with her who bore
Scipio the highth of Rome. With tract oblique
At first, as one who sought access, but feared
To interrupt, sidelong he works his way.
As when a ship by skilful steersman wrought,

Nigh river's mouth or foreland, where the wind
Veers oft, as oft so steers, and shifts her sail,
So varied he, and of his tortuous train
Curled many a wanton wreath in sight of Eve,
To lure her eye: she, busied, heard the sound
Of rustling leaves, but minded not, as used
To such disport before her through the field
From every beast; more duteous at her call
Than at Circean call the herd disguised.
He bolder now, uncalled, before her stood,
But as in gaze admiring, oft he bowed
His turret crest and sleek enamelled neck,
Fawning, and licked the ground whereon she trod.
His gentle dumb expression turned at length
The eye of Eve to mark his play.

(IX. 397-527.)

Satan's object is now within reach. Having gained the pleased attention of his victim, it is an easy task by adroit flattery first to lead her to the Tree of Knowledge, and then to overcome her scruples and bring her to taste the fatal fruit. Adam, for the moment horror-struck at Eve's deed, before long consents to share her guilt.

Satan's end is gained; but it is a costly success. From the pure and lofty spirit, once among the greatest in Heaven, from the still noble rebel, sublimely erring through indomitable pride and ambition, and still looking back with yearning to his former happy estate, he has now come to be the mean trickster of Eden, contriving foully against the children of Earth.

The rest of the story may be told in Milton's own prose (Arguments of Books X, XI, and XII): —

Man's transgression known, the guardian Angels forsake Paradise, and return up to Heaven to approve their vigilance, and are approved; God declaring that the entrance of Satan could not be by them prevented. He sends his Son to judge the transgressors; who descends, and gives sentence accordingly; then, in pity, clothes them both, and reascends. Sin and Death, sitting till then at the gates of Hell, by wondrous sympathy feeling the success of Satan in this new World, and the sin by Man there committed, resolve to sit no longer confined in Hell, but to follow Satan, their sire, up to the place of Man: to make the way easier from Hell to this world, to and fro, they pave a broad highway or bridge over Chaos, according to the track which Satan first made; then, preparing for Earth, they meet him, proud of his success, returning to Hell: their mutual gratulation. Satan arrives at Pandemonium: in full assembly relates, with boasting, his success against Man; instead of applause, is entertained with a general hiss by all his audience, transformed, with himself also, suddenly into serpents, according to his doom given in Paradise; then, deluded with a show of the Forbidden Tree springing up before them, they, greedily reaching to take of the fruit, chew dust and bitter ashes. The proceedings of Sin and Death: God foretells the final victory of his Son over them, and the renewing of all things; but, for the present, commands his Angels to make several alterations in the Heavens and Elements. Adam, more and more perceiving his fallen condition, heavily bewails, rejects the condolement of Eve; she persists, and at length appeases him; then, to evade the curse likely to fall on their offspring, proposes to Adam violent ways; which he approves not, but, conceiving better hope, puts her in mind of the late promise made them, that her Seed should be revenged on the serpent, and exhorts her, with him, to seek peace of the offended Deity by repentance and supplication.

The Son of God presents to his Father the prayers of our first parents, now repenting, and intercedes for them; God accepts them, but declares that they must no longer abide in Paradise; sends Michael with a band of Cherubim to dispossess them; but first to reveal to Adam future things; Michael's coming down; Adam shows to Eve certain ominous signs; he discerns Michael's approach; goes out to meet him; the Angel denounces their departure; Eve's lamentation; Adam pleads, but submits; the Angel leads him up to a high hill; sets before him in vision what shall happen till the flood.

The Angel Michael continues, from the flood, to relate what shall succeed; then, in the mention of Abraham, comes by degrees to explain who that Seed of the Woman shall be, which was promised Adam and Eve in the fall; his incarnation, death, resurrection, and ascension; the state of the Church till his second coming; Adam, greatly satisfied and comforted by these relations and promises, descends the hill with Michael; wakens Eve, who all this while had slept, but with gentle dreams composed to quietness of mind and submission; Michael in either hand leads them out of Paradise:

> They, looking back, all the eastern side beheld
> Of Paradise (so late their happy seat)
> Waved over by that flaming brand, the gate
> With dreadful faces thronged and fiery arms.
> Some natural tears they dropped, but wiped them soon:
> The world was all before them where to choose
> Their place of rest, and Providence their guide.
> They, hand in hand, with wandering steps and slow,
> Through Eden took their solitary way.

(XII. 641–649.)

NOTES.

BOOK I.

5. **seat**; *sedes*, 'abode.' Cf. Virgil's '*sedes beatas*' (*Æneid*, VI. 639).

6. **secret**; *secretus*, 'remote'; hence 'mysterious.'

7. **Of Oreb or of Sinai.** The poet seems to be in doubt as to the name of the mountain whereon Moses communed with God. For the reason of his uncertainty see Exod. xix. 20 and Deut. iv. 10. See if with the aid of a gazetteer you can determine which name is correct.

10, 11. **Sion** and **Siloa** occur naturally to the poet as haunts of the Heavenly Muse (whom he elsewhere calls 'Urania'), just as the 'Aonian mount' Helicon, with its stream Aganippe, was the traditional dwelling-place of the classic Muses.

12. **the oracle of God**; the great temple at Jerusalem, which was built on Mount Sion.

16. **rhyme.** In making use of this spelling, Milton evidently draws a deliberate distinction between 'rime' (see *The Verse*, p. 27), the jingle of verse-endings, and 'rhyme,' a general term for verse as distinguished from prose.

25. **argument**; *argumentum*, 'subject.'

26. **assert**; *asserere*, 'vindicate.'

27–34. Milton's simplest motive in the poem is to inquire into the reasons for the existence of sin in a race of beings created by Almighty power. The inquiry begins with the ultimate result of Satan's revolt, and the answer contents itself at first with naming the immediate factor of that result — the Serpent.

'I am sorry that Milton did not always keep separate the sublime Satan and "the infernal serpent,"' says Landor. Why is it not natural that the poet should connect his first mention of man's enemy, with our simplest memory of the story in Genesis? It is the gradual degrading transformation of the 'sublime Satan' into the 'infernal Serpent' which constitutes the absorbing theme of Milton's narrative.

39. **his peers**; the other archangels.

40. **trusted to have equalled**; long a common construction, even with the most careful writers, but now condemned by grammarians. Does it not give a full flavor to Satan's confidence which would be lacking in the commoner construction?

45. **ethereal sky**; the Empyrean, filled with that mysterious substance 'æther,' imagined by the Greek philosophers to be an element more closely allied with fire than with the air of our nearer heavens. Macmillan notes that '"empyreal substance" (I. 117) is exactly equivalent to "ethereal mould" (II. 139).'

57. **witnessed**; 'bore witness to,' or 'beheld'?

63. **darkness visible.** For a similar paradox, see *Il Penseroso*, 79, 80.

68. **urges**; *urgere*, 'press hard upon.'

72. **utter**; probably 'outer,' with reference to its distance from the throne of God.

74. See *Introduction*, pp. 21, 22.

79. Matt. xii. 24.

83. **thence called Satan.** Satan in Hebrew means 'the adversary.' It should be noted, however, that the Hebrew conception of Satan (as in the story of Job) was not of an adversary of God, but of one of his servants to whom is allotted the duty of testing and disciplining mankind. In Milton's conception, however, Satan is a name of reproach, given to the great rebel after his expulsion from Heaven, when his former glorious name was 'rased from the Books of Life.'

107. **study**; *studium*, 'longing.'

114. **empire**; *imperium*, 'power.'

129. **Seraphim.** Milton uses the titles Seraph, Cherub, Prince, Power, etc., somewhat loosely, preferring, as Macaulay notes in his *Essay on Milton*, not to hedge in the imagination by a strictly specific use of details.

152. **Deep**; Chaos. Gen. i. 2. Milton always calls the place by this name. 'Chaos' is the personal ruler of the Deep. See II. 960. 961.

156. **Arch-Fiend.** We have given the word 'fiend' a much less dignified meaning than it originally had.

167. **if I fail not**; *ni fallor*, 'if I mistake not.'

186. **afflicted**; *afflictus*, 'overthrown.'

187. **offend**; *offendere*, 'do violence to.'

193–196. Is it an accident that there is a suggestion of the serpent in this first description of Satan?

198. **Earth-born**; the Giants. The relative clause which follows applies only to them.

202. **Created hugest**, etc. Notice how plainly the unwieldy bulk of the monster is suggested by the lumbering movement of the verse.

208. **Invests**; 'clothes,' or 'beleaguers'?

215. **Heap on himself damnation.** 'We miss one of the most important things about *Paradise Lost*, if we do not see that it has for a subject not only the Fall of Man, but the Fall of Satan, and not merely his first fall from Heaven, but his constant degradation lower and lower, until the absolute wreck of his physical beauty was a true index to the utter evil of his character' (Hale).

228–238. 'All this is too far detailed,' says Ruskin, 'and deals too much with externals; we feel rather the form of the fire-waves than their fury, we walk upon them too securely, and the fuel, the sublimation, smoke, and singeing, seem to me images only of partial combustion; they vary and extend the conception, but they lower the thermometer. Look back if you will, and add to the description the glimmering of the livid flames; the sulphurous hail and red lightning; yet all together, however they overwhelm us with horror, fail of making us thoroughly unendurably hot.' The critic goes on to quote that passage from Dante (*Purgatorio*, xxvi. 4–8) in which the poet, standing between the western sun and the purgatorial fires, 'made, with his shadow, the flames look more ruddy.' 'That is a slight touch: he has not gone to Ætna nor Pelorus for fuel; but we shall not soon recover from it. He has taken our breath away, and leaves us gasping. No smoke or cinders there. Pure, white, hurtling, formless flame; very fire crystal; we cannot make spires nor waves of it, nor divide it, nor walk on it: there is no question about singeing soles of feet. It is "lambent annihilation"' (*Modern Painters*, Part III.). Consider in connection with this criticism Macaulay's comparison: 'The images which Dante employs speak for themselves; they stand simply for what they are. Those of Milton have a signification which is often discernible only to the initiated. Their value depends less on what they distinctly represent than on what they remotely suggest' (*Essay on Milton*).

254. **its.** Milton uses this word only three times, Shakespeare not more than twice as many. Look up its history. Would it not be preferable to 'his' in 572 below?

266. **astonished**; *attonitus*, 'thunderstruck.'

281. **amazed**; 'bewildered,' 'like one in a maze.'

282. **pernicious**; *perniciosus*, 'swiftly destructive.'

288. **Optic glass** was a not uncommon name for the telescope in its early days. In the course of his Italian journey Milton had himself seen **the Tuscan artist**, Galileo.

290. **Valdarno**; the valley of the Arno, within which lies Florence, the home of Galileo.

294. **ammiral.** Milton is fond of using the Italian forms of certain words: *e.g.* 'ammiral' (*ammiraglio*, a flag-ship); 'sovran' (*sovrano*); 'scape' (*scappare*).

303. It is probable that the poet's description of **Vallombrosa,** a beautiful 'shady vale' not far from Florence, is from memory.

307. What is the meaning of **chivalry** in this passage?

307–311. Exod. xiv.

312. **abject**; *abjectus*, 'hurled down.'

315–330. Satan cleverly bestows upon his followers the lofty titles they have forfeited, hoping that the stirring sound may restore to them something of their former confidence; by the light irony of his opening questions he shows that he himself is unabashed; and by a prompt appeal to their soldierly instinct of obedience fairly lifts them out of themselves, or rather back to themselves. The mechanical process of formation in military order is a great help to them in the recovery of their self-possession.

335. **nor did they not**; *neque non.*

339–343. Exod. x.

341. **warping.** Does this word suggest the rate of speed, or the method of formation? Is it possible to exhaust the suggestiveness of such a vivid touch by appeal to synonyms or definitions?

348. **Sultan**; like 'Emperor' in 378 below, is used by Milton in a large rather that a specific sense.

351–355. What historic invasions are alluded to in this simile? The Rhine and the Danube, you must remember, formed the northern boundary of the Roman Empire. Milton has to draw his illustrations from subsequent human events, in order to make his far-off subject significant to human ears.

364–375. Milton here merely appropriates to his use the common belief of the Christian Fathers that the pagan deities were devils in disguise.

372. **religions**; *religiones*, 'rites.'

384. **Their altars by his altar.** 2 Chron. xxxiii. 4–7.

388. **Within his sanctuary.** 2 Kings xxi. 4, 5.

392–396. For scriptural mention of sacrifices by the Israelites to Moloch, see Jer. vii. 31; Psalms, cvi. 36–38.

396–399. 'The **Ammonites** were a people kindred to the Moabites, both tribes being children of Lot. They dwelt to the east of the land of Gilead: **Rabba** was in the southern part of their territory; **Argob**, mentioned in 1 Kings iv. 13 as a part of **Bashan**, was farther north; the **Arnon** rises in the mountains of Gilead, and flows into the Dead Sea. "Utmost" seems to mean near its source' (Hale).

402. **against the temple of God.** 1 Kings xi. 4–7.

403–405. 'The southern part of the Mount of Olives is blasted with infamy, and called the "hill of scandal" (l. 416), the "offensive mountain" (l. 443), and in the Bible the "mount of corruption" (2 Kings xxiii. 13), because it was disgraced by the shrines of false gods. For the same reason the beautiful valley of Hinnom, after it had been converted into a sacred grove for Moloch, became hateful to the Jews, who made it a receptacle for all the filth of the city. It then came to be known as Tophet (from Hebrew *toph*, a drum), because drums were used at the sacrifice to Moloch to drown the children's cries (l. 394), or Gehenna. The word Gehenna is really derived from Hinnom, but obtained a bad meaning, when the valley was defiled, and became a type of hell' (Macmillan).

406. **Chemos** (or Chemosh) was the national god of the Moabites, whose worship, like that of Moloch, was introduced among the Hebrews by Solomon.

411. **the Asphaltic pool**; the Dead Sea, so called from the asphaltic or bituminous deposits which are found upon its shores.

413. **Israel in Sittim.** Num. xxv.

418. **good Josiah.** 2 Kings xxiii. 13, 14.

446. **Thammuz**, the Greek Adonis, according to the fable, was killed on Lebanon by a wild boar, and ever after upon the anniversary of his death the stream which flows from the mountain side, and which bore his name, was colored with his blood.

452–457. Ezek. viii. 14.

458–461. **when the captive ark**, etc. 1 Sam. v. 4. In the succeeding lines the five principal cities of the Philistines are mentioned.

471. **A leper once he lost.** 2 Kings ix. 17.

472. **Ahaz**, etc. 2 Kings xvi. 10, 11.

484. **The calf in Oreb.** Exod. xxxii. **the rebel king**, Jeroboam. 1 Kings xii. 26–29.

490. **Belial.** The English translation of the Bible treats this word as a name; it is properly a common noun, signifying 'baseness.' The American revisers of the Old Testament recommend the substitution of 'base men' for 'sons of Belial.' Mammon is also a common noun, signifying 'wealth.'

495. **Eli's sons.** 1 Sam. ii. 12, 22.

498. **luxurious**; *luxuriosus*, 'lewd.'

498–502. In Milton's day and later there were in London certain well-known bands of roistering young bloods, who roamed the streets at night, committing all imaginable outrage upon tradespeople and wayfarers. See Macaulay, *Hist. Eng.*, Chap. III.

504. **In Gibeah.** Judges xix. 22–25.

508. **Javan's issue.** 'Javan, son of Japhet' (Gen. x. 2) stands for the Greek race; the name being the same word as Ion (older form 'Ιάων), whence Ionians. So Milton in *Samson Agonistes*, 715, 716, calls the Grecian islands 'isles of Javan' (Verity).

The names which follow are to be looked up in the classical reference books.

543. **reign**; *regnum*, 'realm.'

550. **the Dorian mood**; grave, martial music, as distinguished from the lighter Lydian airs (see *L'Allegro*, 136).

557. **solemn touches.** Compare Shakespeare's 'the touches of sweet harmony' (*Merchant of Venice,* V. l. 57).

563. **horrid**; *horridus*, 'bristling.'

573. **since created man**; '*post hominem creatum.*'

575. **that small infantry**; the Pygmies.

577. **Phlegra**; the Thracian plains upon which the wars between the giants and the gods were fought.

580. **Uther's son.** The story of King Arthur had a strong fascination for Milton; indeed, for years his choice of a subject for his great work seems to have hung undecided between the British Arthur and the World's Satan.

583–587. 'Let us understand in the first place that although Milton, in all probability, used those eight names of places with a clear idea of what place was signified by each one, we shall not get the whole good out of the passage when we know so much ourselves. **Aspramont** is six miles north of Nice, **Montalban** was a castle in Languedoc, and so on. Doubtless it is better, other things being equal, to know where these places were, but that knowledge alone does not give us much enjoyment.

'There are, however, the literary allusions; they add an interest. They certainly do add an interest when one has them at his fingers' ends as Milton had. The half-legendary struggles between the Saracen knighthood and the Crusaders, the romantic adventures of the Paladins of Charlemagne, the final sacrifice of the Song of Roland,—these are all called up, vaguely but effectively, by those few lines. And when Aspramont reminds of the great Orlando, and Montalban is the castle of Rinaldo, the passage certainly has grown in meaning. Still, there is more yet to be said. Even the geographical and literary allusions do not make up the whole atmosphere of the lines.

'There is little doubt that to Milton and to many of his readers the mere mention of strange, well-sounding names had a certain effect, wholly aside from the definite ideas brought to mind by them. They have generally a sonorous, magnificent sound, often from their very unfamiliarity,—a half-mysterious, romantic feeling. When they are geographical, the very fact that they are but half known gives a sort of exhilarating, wide-ranging sensation. Indeed, absolute exactness rather interferes with our enjoyment. It is better, just now, to think of Aspramont as a mediæval castle somewhere in the sunny south of France near the exquisite blue of the Mediterranean than to conceive of it more exactly as six miles north of Nice. It is better that the name **Trebisond** should carry our thoughts out beyond the civilization of Europe, along the Black Sea, with ideas of Eastern magnificence, running astray to the rose-gardens of Persia, perhaps, or the southern spurs of the Caucasus' (Hale).

588. **observe**; *observare*, 'do homage to.'

589–600. This is perhaps the most imposing description in Milton.

597. **disastrous.** To grasp its significance in this passage, you will need to look up the primary meaning of the word. The same remark holds true of **remorse** and **passion** (605 below).

618. **all his peers.** Speaking accurately, Satan had no peers in Hell; he alone had been an Archangel in Heaven. The term is used loosely to include those great subordinates who have lately been named.

636. **different**; 'different from yours,' 'peculiar,' hence 'selfish.'

642. **tempted our attempt.** You will find Milton, in common with all other poets of his time, constantly playing upon words. Compare V. 583:

> 'The empyreal host
> Of Angels, by imperial summons called.'

See also V. 869; IX. 1067; X. 588.

646. **close**; *clausus*, 'closed,' 'secret.'

651. **fame**; *fama*, 'rumor.'

652. **Intended to create.** 'The Universe had actually been created since Satan had been cast out of Heaven. The time now, it must be remembered, is eighteen days after the angels had been expelled from Heaven. See VI. 871; I. 50. The six days of creation are said by Raphael, in Book VII., to have followed immediately the expulsion of the rebels' (Hale).

670. Why should not the consultation to determine specific action take place now? In what ways does the building of Pandemonium serve Satan's ends?

671. **the rest entire**; *omne reliquum*, 'all the rest.'

686. **impious**; *impius*, 'unfilial.'

690. **admire**; *admirari*, 'wonder.'

711. **Rose like an exhalation.** Tennyson has made use of the same figure (*Tithonus*, 63):

> 'While Ilion like a mist rose into towers.'

718. **Alcairo**, Cairo. The first syllable is merely the article.

740. **Mulciber**; Vulcan, or, with the Greeks, Hephæstus. His fall is described in Homer (*Iliad*, I. 590–594).

750. **engines**; *ingenia*, 'devices.'

756. **Pandemonium**; *πανδαιμόνιον*, 'the place of all the demons.'

774. **expatiate**; *expatiari*, 'range about.' **confer**, *conferre*, 'discuss' (trans.).

781. **the Indian mount**; the Himalayas.

785. **arbitress**; *arbitra*, 'witness.'

795. **conclave**; *conclave*, 'a chamber.'

797. **frequent**; *frequens*, 'crowded.'

BOOK II.

2. **Ormus**; now Hormuz, was a town upon a small island near the mouth of the Persian Gulf, once noted as a mart for the jewels of India. In 1653, a dozen years and more before the completion of *Paradise Lost*, the East India Company made its first settlements, and the wonders of India began to be known in England.

4. **Showers on her kings**, etc. 'It was the Eastern ceremony, at the coronation of their kings, to powder them with gold-dust and seed-pearls' (Warburton). These royal honors Cleopatra promises the messenger:

> 'I'll set thee in a shower of gold, and hail
> Rich pearls upon thee.' (*Antony and Cleopatra*, II. 5.)

9. **success.** Evidently our modern use of the word would make nonsense here. Look up its original meaning, and note that in our two uses of the verb form we retain both meanings. The noun is again used in 123 below.

10. **imaginations.** The word is used frequently in this sense in the English New Testament, *e.g.* Rom. i. 21; 2 Cor. x. 5.

14. **give for lost**; 'esteem as lost,' 'admit to be lost,' or merely 'relinquish'?

24–35. This seems to be Satan's customary pose before his followers, and in at least one moment of solitude (IV. 91, 92). Probably his more genuine feeling is expressed frankly in that first moment of awakening in Hell (I. 262, 263). — Reduce this present speech of Satan's to bare terms, and see if it contains a logical thought.

The speeches which follow, of Moloch, Belial, Mammon, and Beëlzebub, should be studied somewhat carefully, and a comparison made of the four characters.

51. **sentence**; *sententia*, 'vote.'

67. **Black fire.** Compare I. 64, 182.

75. **proper**; *proprius*, 'one's own.'

76, 77. **descent and fall to us is adverse**, '*i.e.* inconsistent with our nature. It is a proposition with Milton, as to the physical nature of the angels, that they are not, like men, subject to gravitation. The rebel angels had not properly fallen through Chaos into Hell; they had been *driven* down' (Masson).

89. **exercise**; *exercere*, 'torment.'

94. **incense**; *incendere*, 'kindle.'

106. **denounced**; *denuntiare*, 'threaten.'

109. **humane**; *humanus*, 'polished.'

113, 114. Socrates was accused of making 'the worse appear the better reason' (Plato, *Apology*). Milton had in mind probably the Sophists, mere disputants who, like Belial, deliberately varnished fallacies with plausibility.

119–225. In the first part of his speech Belial takes up, one by one, the points which Moloch has made, and replies to each in detail. Later (187–225), he brings forward his own theory.

139. **ethereal mould.** See note on I. 45 above. The subtle fire of which the Heavenly substance is made, and which Milton calls indifferently 'ethereal' and 'empyreal,' would, says Belial, easily overcome and free itself from the 'baser fire' of Hell.

158, 159. **whom his anger saves to punish endless.** 'The Devil,' says Sir Thomas Browne, 'were it in his power, would do the like [destroy himself]; which being impossible, his miseries are endless, and he suffers most in that attribute . . . his immortality.'

181, 182. **the sport and prey of racking whirlwinds.** Vergil's '*rapidis ludibria ventis.*'

184. **converse**; *conversari*, 'dwell together.'

185. Compare *Hamlet*, I. 5. 77.

210. **Supreme.** 'This throwing back of the accent in words like "supreme," "extreme," "complete," "obscure" (cf. 132), is

usual in Milton (and Shakespeare), when they precede a monosyllable, or a noun accented on the first syllable' (Verity).

224. **For happy**; 'as to the chances of happiness it affords.'

227. **ignoble ease and peaceful sloth.** 'These words,' says Landor, 'are spoken by the poet in his own person, very improperly; they would have suited the character of any fallen angel, but the reporter of the occurrence ought not to have delivered such a sentence.'

255, 256. **preferring hard liberty**, etc. Cook quotes from *Prometheus Bound*, 966, 967:

> 'I would not barter — learn thou soothly that —
> My suffering for thy service.'

299–309. **Which when Beëlzebub perceived**, etc. 'Observe how Milton reserves the decisive speech for the great angel, Beëlzebub, the chief next to Satan, and already privately advised of his plans. In the preceding speeches Milton intended, doubtless, to represent poetically three very common types of statesmanship. Some men, in emergencies, take the Moloch view of affairs, which recommends boisterous action at all hazards; others take the Belial view, which recommends slothful and epicurean acquiescence; and others the Mammon view, which believes in the material industries and the accumulation of wealth. The angels in the Council are evidently inclining to Belial's view, or to that as modified by Mammon, when a greater statesman than any of the three strikes in with a specific plan of action, not vague and blustering like Moloch's, but subtly adapted to the exigencies' (Masson).

322. **reserved**; *reservare*, 'restrain.'

330. **determined**; *determinare*, 'set bounds to.'

375. **original**; *origo*, 'progenitor.'

379, 380. **first devised by Satan**, etc. See I. 650–656 above.

404. **tempt**; *temptare*, 'essay.'

407. **uncouth**; used in its older sense.

410. **The happy isle**; not the earth, but the World, or Universe, of which alone the fallen angels have knowledge.

412. **stations**; *stationes*, 'guards.' This passage Landor calls 'such a torrent of eloquence as there is nowhere else in the region of poetry, although *strict* and *thick*, in v. 412, sound unpleasantly.'

434. Why do we find **convex** here, and 'concave' in 635 below?

438. Notice the dim grandeur of the suggestion in such phrases applied to chaos as **the void profound**, 'the palpable obscure,' and 'the vast abrupt.'

439. **unessential**; 'unsubstantial.'

456. **intend**; 'attend to,' 'consider.'

464. **Through all the coasts**, etc. '*Coasts*, used now of the sea-line, but in Milton's day more generally in the meaning *country*. There is nothing in the origin of the word to make the expression "sea-coast" tautological' (Hale).

471. **opinion**; as frequently in Shakespeare, 'reputation.'

496–505. Mr. Hale suggests: 'This reflection of Milton's may have been called forth by the impossibility of the Puritan leaders coming to any good understanding after the death of Cromwell. He may have felt that had they shown a firm united front, the Restoration would not have come.'

528. **sublime**; *sublimis*, 'aloft.'

531, 532. **shun the goal with rapid wheels**; '*metaque fervidis evitata rotis*' (Horace, Ode I.).

542. **Alcides**; Hercules.

558–561. This contemptuous reference to theological discussion is not without pathos as a confession, from the poet's own experience, of the futility of polemic controversy. Yet the later books of this poem are by no means free from just this sort of discussion. (See III. 96–128; V. 524–534.)

592. **Serbonian bog.** Herodotus mentions this lake, which lay very near the sea, on the northeast coast of Egypt. Long ago it vanished into the sands.

597. **The damned** whose fate is here described are of course not Satan's angelic followers, but the offspring of Adam. The passage (596–616) is therefore a digression.

600. **starve**; allied with the German *sterben*. Hale says that 'in some English dialects it means "to die of cold."'

621. Cook has the following note on this verse:

Lowell comments: 'Milton, like other great poets, wrote some bad verses, and it is wiser to confess that they are so than to conjure up some unimaginable reason why the reader should accept them as the better for their badness. Such a bad verse is

Rocks, caves, lakes, *fens*, bogs, *dens* and shapes of death, which might be cited to illustrate Pope's

And ten low words oft creep in one dull line.'

But Burke says (*Sublime and Beautiful*, Part 5, Sec. 7): 'Here is displayed the force of union, . . . which yet would lose the greatest part of the effect if they were not the

Rocks, caves, lakes, fens, bogs, dens, and shades—of *Death.*

This . . . raises a very great degree of the sublime; and this sublime is raised yet higher by what follows, a "universe of death."'

What impression do the verses make upon you? Landor, quoting lines 614–621, says: 'It is impossible to refuse the ear its satisfaction at' them.

641, 642. The merchants are described as sailing through the Indian Ocean southward to the Cape of Good Hope.

647. **impaled**; 'fenced in.'

650. 'Milton's figure of *Sin* is own sister to Spenser's *Error* and Phineas Fletcher's *Hamartia*, or Sin; their common origin being the classical accounts of Scylla, notably Ovid's (*Met.* XIV.) and Vergil's (*Æneid*, III.). It is, therefore, as a study in a familiar style, not as a fresh creation, that the picture should be viewed; comparison it challenges and bears, originality it does not claim. So with his figure of Death. . . . The basis of the allegory of Sin and Death lies, appropriately, in Scripture: "Then when lust hath conceived, it bringeth forth sin; and sin, when it is finished, bringeth forth death," James i. 15' (Verity).

693. **conjured**; *conjurare*, 'swear together.'

706. **deform**; *deformis*, 'shapeless.'

709. **Ophiuchus**; 'Serpent-bearer,' a constellation in the northern heavens.

721, 722. **never but once more**. When was this to be? See 1 Cor. xv. 26; Heb. ii. 14.

755–758. What classic myth does this recall?

833. **purlieus**. Look up the history of the word, and that of **buxom**, 842 below.

889. **redounding**; *redundare*, 'overflow.'

891–916. 'It would be difficult,' says Masson, 'to quote a passage from any poet so rich in purposely accumulated perplexities.

learned or poetical, or in which so much care is taken, and so successfully, to compel the mind to a rackingly intense conception of sheer Inconceivability.'

895. **ancestors of Nature**; of nature as known to us in our Universe.

943–947. **Arimaspian.** According to Herodotus, the Arimaspians were a one-eyed race, dwellers in the remote North, who carried on fierce feud with the gryphons, or griffins, a mythical creature half eagle and half lion.

964, 965. **the name of Demogorgon**; Demogorgon himself; a Latinism.

1001–1006. 'This is the first distinct intimation to Satan that the new universe of Man had actually been created. He had guessed so before leaving Hell, but it was still only a guess in his speech to Chaos a few lines back' (Masson).

1029, 1030. **the utmost orb of this frail World**; the outermost star, or the outer spherical shell of the Universe?

1046. **Weighs**; 'balances.'

1051–1053. *i.e.* 'The World, or Universe, is as insignificant beside the Empyrean from which it hangs, as the smallest star beside the moon.'